ABE LINCOLN
LOG CABIN TO WHITE HOUSE

It is difficult for anyone growing up today to understand just how harsh Abraham Lincoln's childhood was. Often shoeless and poorly clothed, he was barely sheltered against the bitter elements and even spent one winter in an open lean-to. Educated only in fits and starts (and according to the "blab school" method of teaching, where students of every grade recited lessons aloud in a single schoolroom), he was also required to perform heavy labor from an early age.

But Abe Lincoln surmounted these and many other barriers, and all the while he kept his gentle nature and his sense of humor. This book tells the story of a very special man who rose from a background of poverty and ignorance to attain the highest office in the land and the enduring love of the American people.

ABE LINCOLN
LOG CABIN TO WHITE HOUSE

By Sterling North

Random House New York

For Gladys with love
— S. N.

Copyright © 1956 by Sterling North. Text copyright renewed 1984 by Gladys North. All rights reserved under International and Pan-American Copyright Conventions. Published in the United States by Random House, Inc., New York, and simultaneously in Canada by Random House of Canada Limited, Toronto.

Library of Congress Cataloging-in-Publication Data:
North, Sterling.
  Abe Lincoln.
  (A Landmark book)
  SUMMARY: A biography of Abraham Lincoln, focusing on his childhood spent in poverty on the Midwestern frontier and chronicling his rise to the presidency and the highlights of his tenure.
  1. Lincoln, Abraham, 1809–1865—Juvenile literature. 2. Lincoln, Abraham, 1809–1865—Childhood and youth—Juvenile literature. 3. Presidents—United States—Biography—Juvenile literature. [1. Lincoln, Abraham, 1809–1865. 2. Presidents] I. Title. E457.905.N63 1987 973.7'092'4 [B] [92] 87-4654 ISBN: 0-394-89179-1 (trade); 0-394-90361-7 (lib. bdg.)

Manufactured in the United States of America
1 2 3 4 5 6 7 8 9 0

Contents

ABE LINCOLN
LOG CABIN TO WHITE HOUSE

Nancy's Boy Baby

It [the story of my early life] can all be condensed into a single sentence and that sentence you will find in Gray's Elegy—*"The short and simple annals of the poor."*

A. LINCOLN

Nine-year-old Dennis Hanks sped down the path that led to the Lincoln cabin. Leaping ice-crusted puddles and avoiding the frozen ruts, he skimmed along the curving trail that wandered through the brush-covered hills bordering Nolin Creek.

It was Sunday, February 12, 1809, a day that was to become famous in American history. But on that cold winter morning, Dennis was only aware that a boy baby had been born to Tom and Nancy Hanks Lincoln—a son named Abraham.

Dennis often came down this road to visit the Lincolns. He and Nancy Lincoln were first cousins. Both had been reared by their kindly aunt and uncle, Tom and Betsy Sparrow. No wonder the Lincolns had wanted the Sparrows to be the first to see the new baby.

Blue wood-smoke was rising from the chimney of the Lincoln cabin as Dennis raced into the clearing, the tail of his coonskin cap streaming in the wind. He wondered what little Abe would look like. Dennis didn't think much of babies in general, but maybe Nancy's would be something special.

As the boy lifted the latch and stepped into the fire-lit, one-room cabin, he saw for the first time, lying there beside the tired but smiling Nancy, the homely baby who would one day become America's most beloved president.

Years later, when Dennis Hanks was an old man, he liked to tell the story of that frosty morning. Perhaps he mixed a few of his facts and invented a few others as old men sometimes do. But listeners never forgot the tale as he told it:

"Nancy was layin' thar in a pole bed lookin'

purty happy. Tom'd built up a good fire and throwed a b'ar skin over the kivers to keep 'em warm."

Betsy Sparrow was scurrying about, doing everything a woman could for mother and child. She washed little Abe and put "a yaller flannen petticoat an' a linsey shirt on him, an' cooked some dried berries with wild honey fur Nancy, an' slicked things up."

Nancy let Dennis hold the baby, and the boy noticed that the infant's face looked like "red cherry-pulp, squeezed dry, in wrinkles."

"Be keerful, Dennis," Nancy said, "fur you air the fust boy he's ever seen."

After a few minutes Dennis handed the crying baby to his aunt Betsy Sparrow, saying, "Aunt, take him! He'll never come to much." The Lincolns and particularly the Hankses were humble people who never could have imagined that this child would one day be a great and famous man.

Little Abe lay in his cradle that first year needing nothing but food and warmth and love. What did he see from where he lay? Firelight. A spinning wheel turning. The gentle face of his mother bending over him. Perhaps the coarse, black hair and swarthy face of Tom Lincoln as he took his hunting rifle from its pegs above the fireplace. Often another face appeared—that of his two-year-old sister, Sarah, looking tenderly at her baby brother; rocking him; laughing when Abe smiled; constantly asking when he would be big enough to talk and to play with her.

And the second year? Walking as best he could, holding his sister's hand, he must have visited the spring of clear water for which the farm was named. Out of a little cave poured the crystal stream. It ran between mossy stones. Then it disappeared mysteriously into the earth, making a sound like music.

When he grew to manhood, Lincoln remembered nothing of Sinking Spring Farm, his birthplace on the South Fork of Nolin Creek, near Hodgenville, Kentucky. His first memories were of another farm not many miles away to which the family moved when he was two years old. Once again Thomas Lincoln built a rough log cabin, this time in the fertile valley of Knob Creek, beneath the shadow of a great ridge known as

Muldraugh's Hill.

"It didn't seem no time till Abe was runnin' 'round in buckskin moccasins an' breeches, a tow-linen shirt an' coonskin cap," Dennis Hanks was later to recall. "Abe never give Nancy no trouble after he could walk except to keep him in clothes. Most o' the time we went b'ar foot. . . . An' Abe was right out in the woods, about as soon's he was weaned, fishin' in the crick . . . goin' on coon hunts with Tom an' me an' the dogs; follerin' up bees to find bee trees, an' drappin' corn fur his pappy. Mighty interestin' life fur a boy, but thar was a good many chances he wouldn't live to grow up."

Abe Lincoln seems to have had similar memories of those years. "My earliest recollection is of the Knob Creek place. . . . Our farm was composed of three fields which lay in the valley surrounded by high hills and deep gorges. . . . One Saturday afternoon the other boys planted the corn in what we called 'the big field'—it contained seven acres—and I dropped the pumpkin seed. I dropped two seeds every other hill and every other row. The next Sunday morning there came a big rain in the hills; it did not rain a drop in the valley, but

7

the water coming down through the gorges, washed ground, corn, pumpkin seeds and all clear off the field."

In one such flood as this, Abe fell into the creek and might have drowned. Luckily his friend and playmate, Austin Gollaher, was on hand to hold out a long branch and drag him safely to shore.

It was here on the Knob Creek farm that Abe gained his first glimpse of the larger world. Down the Cumberland Trail, which passed the cabin door, came travelers of all sorts—peddlers, pioneers seeking new land, even slaves in chains. Once Abe gave a fish he had caught in the creek to a discharged soldier hobbling home from the War of 1812. The big-eared Lincoln boy listened, watched, and wondered. He has been described as a spidery lad with his fair share of mischief. But even at so young an age he was willing and eager to learn.

In time there came to the community a schoolteacher named Zachariah Riney. He taught in a dirt-floored log cabin where every student studied aloud in the noisy "blab school" manner of the frontier. Abe continued to read aloud to himself for the rest of his life.

Thomas Lincoln had little respect for "book larnin'." Abraham later wrote that his father had been "a wandering laboring boy" who had grown up "literally without education." Tom was a good hunter, a fair carpenter, and a hard-working but unsuccessful farmer. He could hold any listener's attention when he told a story. However, this thickset frontiersman could but "bunglingly sign his own name" and he scoffed at "eddication."

Many remembered that Nancy Hanks Lincoln, despite the poverty and illiteracy of the Hanks and Sparrow family background, was a woman of rare tenderness and native intelligence. Some say she could read and write, but this is unlikely. However, it was undoubtedly this greatly loved mother of Abraham and Sarah who insisted that her children be given at least a few months of schooling.

In 1816, Nancy noticed that Thomas Lincoln was becoming restless. Once again he was in danger of losing his land because other men claimed it. Besides, he found it hard for a poor farmer without slaves to make a living in a slave-holding state. North of the Ohio River lay fertile and almost unpopulated Indiana. Thomas argued that here was a great opportunity—a man could stake out a new farm and get a fresh start.

Already uprooted three times in ten years of married life, Nancy Lincoln must have wondered if Thomas would ever be satisfied. This was the coldest year the frontier had ever experienced, a year which was called by the pioneers "Eighteen-Hundred-and-Froze-to-Death." By the time Tom came back from scouting the new country, it would be late in the autumn, a dangerous season in which to start into the wilderness with two small children. Sometimes Nancy must have wept as she lay alone in the dark cabin with the wind whistling down the chimney.

But to Abe, the new move must have seemed an exciting promise of adventure. Perhaps he climbed the high bluff behind the cabin to look northward across miles of frost-tinted woodland toward distant Indiana, whose very name suggested Indians. Certainly there would be bears aplenty. But what had Abe to fear? Soon he would be eight years old and able to handle a gun or axe almost as well as a full-grown man.

Shielding his eyes against the October sun, Abe wondered if that trace of blue he could see so far away to the north was part of the sky. Or was it the mighty Ohio River, on whose far shore lay the promised land of Indiana?

2

The "Half-Face" Camp

We reached our new home about the time the State [of Indiana] came into the Union. It was a wild region, with many bears and other wild animals still in the woods. There I grew up.

A. LINCOLN

When Tom Lincoln returned in November he told Nancy and the children that he had staked out a farm of one hundred sixty acres near Pigeon Creek several miles north of the Ohio River. No doubt he told them of the rich land and the abundance of deer and wild turkeys. But perhaps he failed to mention that the nearest water fit to drink was from a distant spring, or that the forest was filled with bears, wolves, panthers, and wildcats, while the nearby swamps bred malaria.

It was true that in Indiana the government surveys made land titles more dependable than they were in Kentucky. And some of the soil *was* fertile. But even Tom Lincoln might well have worried about moving his wife and children at the onset of winter to a patch of uncleared wilderness where as yet there was not even a cabin for their shelter.

We must again trust the account of Dennis Hanks, the only eyewitness to record the departure of the Lincoln family for Indiana:

"Nancy emptied the shucks out o' the tow-linen ticks, an' I piled everything they had wuth takin' on the backs o' two pack hosses. Tom could make new pole beds an' puncheon tables an' stools easier 'n he could carry 'em. Abe toted a gun."

After two days of traveling, the Lincolns reached the south bank of the Ohio River opposite the mouth of Anderson Creek on the Indiana shore. Boarding a makeshift ferry, they crossed the river at this wide and beautiful bend, landing at the farm of a man named Posey. Here they plunged into the woods, clearing a trail slowly and painfully for sixteen endless miles through the unbro-

13

ken wilderness to the new farm.

The virgin timber through which they struggled still held some of its autumn leaves. The poplars and beeches shimmered with their last tatters of gold; a few maples were still crimson; and the shagbark hickories scattered leaves of buckskin and a shower of hickory nuts on the forest floor. The gnarled oaks, slowest of all to give up their leaves, were clothed in russet and brown. Majestic sycamores, their gray trunks dappled with light, towered along the banks of every stream. And the warm tints of the sassafras told where one might dig spicy roots for sassafras tea. Everywhere, through walnut, sweet gum, ash, and elm trees, ran the tangled vines of the wild grapes which hung in frosted purple clusters along yellowed leaves. Mighty trees, which had been towering here since before the time of man, spread endlessly beyond any possible horizon. "Nothing but woods, woods, woods, as far as the world extends."

In the shadows of this forest lurked no unfriendly Indians. No tribes were on the warpath in southern Indiana in 1816. But Abe, who had kept his powder dry while crossing the Ohio, maintained a sharp watch as the Lincolns moved slowly through the trees. He could not have forgotten that he was named for his grandfather who had been killed by an Indian back in Kentucky. Abe's father had often told that story. Perhaps he told it again as they huddled beside the campfire with the dark woods looming around them, while a far-off wolf howled to the stars.

That earlier Abraham Lincoln, Abe's grandsire, had been a friend of Daniel Boone. He had moved from Virginia through the mountains to Kentucky in 1782. He and his wife, Bathsheba, together with their three sons and two daughters, settled on the Green River in Kentucky, where they filed claim to more than two thousand acres.

One day in May 1786, when Abe's grandfather and his sons were working in the field, a shot rang out from the nearby woods and old Abraham fell to the ground. In a few moments he was dead. Tom Lincoln was a small boy of eight at the time. While his two older brothers ran for help, little Tom, brave but terrified, stood beside the body of his father. He turned to see an Indian dart from his ambush and come racing toward him across the field.

Would the Indian take him captive? Would he kill him on the spot? Tom stared with fascination at a shining medal that dangled on the Indian's breast. A moment later he heard another shot—this time from the stockade. Just below the medal, blood oozed from a bullet hole as the warrior pitched forward at Tom's feet. Tom's brothers were sharpshooters who could hit the eye of a squirrel.

With old Abraham dead, the family had scattered to the four winds, winds that had blown Tom all the way to Indiana.

Young Abe drew closer to the fire. Another wolf now answered his lonesome brother. And as the firelight flickered a distant panther screamed, sending icy shivers along the Lincolns' spines.

When they reached the new farm, the only way in which they could identify it was that Tom had piled brush at the four corners of the one hundred sixty acres. Abe and his father quickly threw up a half-faced camp, a hunter's shelter fourteen feet wide and perhaps as deep. It was framed with poles, thatched with bark, and was entirely open on the southern side, where a log fire was kept burning night and day. Leaves were their floor and also their bed in this man-made cave. Except when the rain, snow, or smoke swirled into their hut, the Lincolns had a home almost as snug as the hollow trees where the squirrels lived.

Tom Lincoln soon began to build a better cabin. But all through that miserable winter, Abe, Sarah, and their parents huddled in their half-faced shelter.

Luckily, game was plentiful. They did not lack for food. But water was a problem. One of Abe's jobs for many years was to make frequent trips to the spring a mile away. He also helped to cut logs for the new cabin. At least once he brought meat to the table.

Long afterward, as though he were telling of some other boy, Abraham Lincoln wrote:

"A., though very young, was large of his age, and had an axe put into his hands at once; and from that till within his twentythird year, he was almost constantly handling that most useful instrument—less, of course, in plowing and harvesting seasons. At this place A. took an early start as a hunter, which was never much improved afterwards. (A few days before the completion of his eighth year, in the absence of his father, a flock of wild turkeys approached the new log-cabin, and A. with a rifle gun, standing inside, shot through a crack, and killed one of them. He has never since pulled a trigger on any larger game.)"

April came at last with its surging rush of leaves and flowers, up the Mississippi River, up the Ohio, and finally up Pigeon Creek. It swept over the half-faced camp and the unfinished Lincoln cabin in a foaming blizzard of white blossoms. It crept through the new grass, leaving the purple stain of violets and the gold of the buttercups. Corn and "garden sass" were planted in the enlarged clearing. But bears came to eat the pigs, as Lincoln recalled in a bit of verse:

When first my father settled here,
'Twas then the frontier line:
The panther's scream, filled night with fear
And bears preyed on the swine.

In the autumn of 1817, a little less than one year after the arrival of the Lincolns, the lonely clearing on Pigeon Creek was made less lonely by the arrival of Thomas and Betsy Sparrow and the lively Dennis Hanks. Of course, the Sparrows were foster parents to both Nancy Lincoln and her cousin Dennis. Here in Indiana they were usually known as the "Father and Mother of Mrs. Lincoln."

The Sparrows nested in "that darne little half-face camp," as Dennis always called it. The Lincolns began living in their new cabin—a log house eighteen by twenty feet with a loft. Here Nancy could set up her spinning wheel, cook her corn dodgers in a real fireplace, and sleep in a pole bed. Here once again she could have a puncheon table and stools. But Tom Lincoln failed to furnish the cabin with a slab door or with greased paper to cover the window hole. Cold winds could sweep around the skins which hung at the openings. The floor was the bare ground. The cracks between the logs were unchinked. Even the roof was left unfinished. It is little wonder that pioneers often died young.

Dennis Hanks recalled that "We all hunted pretty much all the time. Especially so when we got tired of work—which was very often I will assure you."

While the Lincolns shivered in their unfinished cabin during the winter of 1817–18, the Sparrows and Dennis Hanks froze in the half-faced camp. Six acres were cleared for the spring planting of 1818, but both families still lived largely on wild game and berries and nuts.

With the next autumn came the most dreaded disease of the frontier, the mysterious "milk sickness," which killed cows and human beings alike. Whatever the nature of this scourge, Thomas and Betsy Sparrow soon lay sick in that open hut with Nancy nursing them as best she could. They died on their couch of leaves, like wounded animals gone to earth.

Not long after Tom Lincoln had finished their crude coffins and lowered them side by side into their graves, Nancy took to her bed. The nearest doctor lived thirty-five miles away. Even if Tom had tried to reach him, it would have done little good. No living human being knew any cure for milk sickness.

The leaves again were brilliant and the sky was blue with autumn when the gentle and humble mother of Abraham and Sarah called the children to her side. She made them promise to be good and to be kind to each other. Then she died very quietly, and the cabin was motherless and the spinning wheel silent.

Said Dennis Hanks, "O Lord, O Lord, I'll never furgit the mizry in that little green-log cabin in the woods when Nancy died!

"Me 'n' Abe helped Tom make the coffin. He tuk a log left over from buildin' the cabin, an' I helped him whipsaw it into planks an' plane 'em. Me 'n' Abe held the planks while Tom bored holes an' put 'em together, with pegs Abe'd whittled. . . . 'Pears to me like Tom was always makin' a coffin fur someone. We laid Nancy close to the deer-run in the woods. Deer was the only wild critters the women wasn't afeered of. Abe was som'er's 'round nine years old, but he never got over the mizable way his mother died."

21

It was peaceful there. The leaves of autumn and the snow of winter drifted down almost without a whisper. It was a place where Abe could go when he felt sorrowful and alone.

3

The New Mother

Abe was a good boy . . . never gave me a cross word or look . . . he was kind to everybody and to everything. . . . His mind and mine, what little I had, seemed to run together—move in the same channel.
SARAH BUSH LINCOLN

For more than a year after Nancy Lincoln died, twelve-year-old Sarah did the cooking for her father, ten-year-old Abe, and Dennis Hanks. Life was "plumb miserable" in that half-finished cabin there in the little clearing at the forks of Pigeon Creek.

It worried Tom that no funeral service had been said over Nancy and the Sparrows. It helped a little when Parson Elkin of Hardin County, Kentucky, happened by one day and agreed to say the

23

right words over the mounds of earth near the deer path. Abe and Sarah, Dennis and Tom bowed their heads while the preacher read the service for the dead. Ashes to ashes and dust to dust!

But no words can ever counter the loss of someone beloved. Nancy was no longer there to give them courage and sympathy; to card and spin and weave; to make soap and candles and hominy. In their despair the family became ragged and unkempt, careless about their cleanliness.

With another autumn came the first anniversary of Nancy's death. No longer able to bear his loneliness, Tom Lincoln made a trip back to Kentucky. While he was gone, the three young people lived alone in the cabin, more forlorn than ever. When the wind moaned through the trees on a dark night and the autumn leaves rattled and scratched across the hand-split shakes of the roof, they sometimes wondered if a panther was seeking to claw his way into the cabin.

In Elizabethtown, Tom Lincoln wasted no time in going to the home of Sarah Bush Johnston, a woman whom he had courted before marrying Nancy Hanks. Sarah's husband, Daniel Johnston, had died, leaving her with three children: Elizabeth, Matilda, and John. Tom's motherless pair and Sarah's fatherless trio were of much the same age and of similar need.

According to the story of one witness, Tom said to Sarah, "Well, *Miss* Johnston, I have no wife, and you have no husband. I came a-purpose to marry you. I knowed you from a gal, and you knowed me from a boy. I have no time to lose; and, if you are willin', let it be done straight off."

And Sarah is said to have replied:

"Tommy, I know you well, and have no objection to marrying you; but I cannot do it straight off, as I owe some debts that must first be paid."

That didn't discourage Tom Lincoln. He paid the debts, and on the following day, which was December 2, 1819, these two were married.

It was a great wonder to Abe, Sarah, and Dennis when a "four-hoss wagon-load o' goods—feather pillers an' chists o' drawers, an' a flax-wheel an' a soap kittle, an' cookin' pots an' pewter dishes," not to mention a smiling new mother, plus a new brother and two new sisters, pulled into the foreyard of the cabin at Pigeon Creek.

Sarah Bush Lincoln must have been a woman of character. Otherwise she would have turned around and started back home. She had left a comfortable, clean, well-furnished little house. Here she found a dirt-floored cabin without windows or doors, a few pieces of split-log furniture, cornhusk mattresses, and a pole bed. Abe, Sarah, and Dennis were far from clean.

As Dennis later admitted, "I reckon we was all purty ragged and dirty when she got thar. The fust thing she did was to tell me to tote one o' Tom's carpenter benches to a place outside the door, near the hoss-trough. Then she had me 'n' Abe 'n' John Johnston, her boy, fill the trough with spring water. She put out a big gourd full o' soft soap, an' another one to dip water with, an' told us boys to wash up fur dinner. You jist naturally had to be somebody when Aunt Sairy was around."

Abe and his sister took an immediate liking to their handsome and affectionate stepmother. She is the "angel mother" whom Lincoln remembered so fondly all of his life. With good-natured efficiency she went after the tangled hair and grimy

26

clothes of her new children. She scrubbed the cabin, and set Tom to laying a puncheon floor. No moth-eaten bearskin hanging in the doorway would satisfy Sarah. She insisted on a weather-tight slab door with leather hinges. While Tom put up additional pole beds, Sarah emptied the old ticks, washed them, filled them with fresh cornhusks, and over these put her feather beds and clean bedding. She did the same for the boys' beds in the loft. Lime was purchased, and the walls and ceilings were whitewashed. The unbelievable bureau which had "cost forty-five dollars" when purchased in Kentucky gleamed in dark magnificence in one corner. Abe began feeling and looking "more human."

This new stepmother, who was to encourage Abe in all his ambitions, seems to have been a woman of tenderness, charm, and courage. A granddaughter of Sarah described her as "a very tall Woman, Straight as an Indian, fair Complection . . . very handsome, Sprightly talkative and proud, Wore her Hair curled till Gray." A photograph taken late in life shows her still attractive, with sweetness shining from her old face. She kept the cabin spotless and ruled her large, mixed brood with affection, humor, and tolerance. She and Abe often shared their laughter.

It must have been a wonderful and slightly boisterous Christmas on that December 25, 1819, when Sarah fixed the wild turkey and venison for all those hungry children. And Tom Lincoln must have added a few thankful words to his usual brief blessing as they sat with bowed heads around the long puncheon table loaded with a savory Christmas feast in a clean cabin that was no longer motherless.

4

A Frontier Education

There were some schools, so called; but no qualification was ever required of a teacher, beyond "readin', writin' and cipherin' " to the Rule of Three. . . . There was absolutely nothing to excite ambition for education.
A. LINCOLN

Almost everyone who knew Abe Lincoln during his barefooted boyhood in southern Indiana remembered two things about him: that his buckskin breeches were always too short for his long legs, exposing at least six inches of sharp, blue shinbone, and that he was always carrying a book.

That meant that Abe was growing physically and mentally—physically until he became in his late teens a powerful young giant able to "sink an axe deeper" than any man in his neighborhood.

Mentally he perhaps was no prodigy, but certainly the quickest-witted and best-informed boy in many a mile, able to hold the attention of children or adults when he climbed a stump to imitate the arm-waving oratory of backwoods preachers and politicians. At such times he sent his admiring audiences into gales of laughter. But he could also be serious, repeating parts of sermons he had heard at church or whole pages from books he had read.

He was both shy and a show-off; full of jokes and tricks and yet deeply thoughtful and sometimes sad; gentle by nature and yet a fighter when thoroughly aroused.

Throughout his entire life, even after he had been elected to the presidency, Lincoln mourned his lack of formal schooling and was humble about the additional learning he finally acquired from his own study and reading. Rising from a background of poverty and ignorance, struggling virtually unaided and alone, Abraham Lincoln finally achieved deeper wisdom than millions of men who have been given every educational advantage.

As Lincoln expressed it, he went to school "by littles." He studied under five teachers—two in

Kentucky and three in Indiana—but his entire schooling amounted to less than one year. His three Indiana schoolmasters were named Crawford, Dorsey, and Sweeney (or Swaney). His schoolbooks were probably Webster's blueback speller, Pike's *Arithmetic,* and the Bible.

All of these frontier "subscription schools" were very much alike. Tuition for each pupil was usually paid in farm produce such as ham or cornmeal or in coonskins. The school building itself was a log cabin. Greased paper over the window holes let in a few shafts of dim light. The split-log benches were not too comfortable. And although the blazing logs in the fireplace nearly scorched the teacher and the students in the front row, the students in the back rows shivered on cold days, finding it difficult to hold a quill pen in half-frozen fingers.

During one session Lincoln walked four and one-half miles each way every day. In pleasant weather he probably enjoyed his tramp through the woods, watching squirrels scurrying up the oaks and hickories, or seeing a white-tailed deer bounding away through the trees.. But often in winter he must have arrived soaked to the skin with rain or melting snow. Dennis Hanks wrote of those days: "Moccasins wasn't no putection ag'inst the wet. Birch bark, with hickory bark soles, stropped on over yarn socks, beat buckskin all holler, fur snow." But wet feet must have added further misery to that nine-mile round trip in stormy weather.

Nevertheless, school meant so much to Abe that he tried to make the most of every precious day. Nathaniel Grigsby, a fellow student, said that Abe was always at school early, always at the head of his class, and passed all other pupils rapidly in his studies. He was the best speller in his school and once in a spell-down helped a girl spell "d-e-f-i-e-d" by quietly pointing to his eye when she hesitated after the letter *f*.

Indiana, like Kentucky, followed the blab school method of teaching. The continuous babble, as children of all ages studied their various lessons aloud, made the school sound from a distance like a large hive of bees. Inside it roared like a political convention. The teachers "licked learning" into their pupils with the aid of a hickory stick. A stupid child was likely to be sent to the corner and made to wear the cone-shaped dunce's hat. Sometimes the schoolmaster had to fight some big, sullen boy at the start of the term to prove who *was* the master. It's a wonder that anyone learned anything.

Mr. Crawford tried to teach manners to the children by having a student enter the room as though he were a stranger to be properly introduced to the other pupils. At Mr. Dorsey's school Abe learned to write a beautiful clear script and to read fluently. The first penmanship that we have in Lincoln's own hand is the following verse:

Abraham Lincoln his hand and pen
he will be good but God knows When

At both the Dorsey and Sweeney schools he wrote essays against cruelty to animals—a fact so completely astonishing to the rough and tough frontiersmen that several of his schoolmates never forgot those pleas for gentle treatment of dumb animals. Throughout life a lover of poetry, Lincoln tried his skill at writing verse at both of the last two schools he attended, and for many years thereafter.

In an early copybook he wrote these rather sad lines:

> *Time What an emty vapor tis*
> *and days how swift they are*
> *swift as an indian arrow*
> *fly on like a shooting star*
> *the presant moment Just, is here*
> *then slides away in haste*
> *that we can never say they're ours*
> *but only say they're past.*

Several of Lincoln's old neighbors later recalled that Abe was "lazy," that he liked his pay and his dinner better than his work. Dennis Hanks, who always greatly admired Lincoln, nevertheless confessed that Abe was "very lazy. . . . He was always reading, Scribbling, writing, ciphering, writing Poetry." Abe told a nearby farmer that his father had taught him how to work, but not how to like it.

Actually young Lincoln, sprouting in mind and

body like a tall hickory sapling, needed much of his energy just to keep up with the growing process. And more to the point—he *was* working. In addition to all the manual labor he performed from about his eighth year on, he was now struggling to educate himself. To uneducated people such as most of these cabin dwellers, reading and studying were never considered "work." They had no way of knowing that one of the most mentally active young men in southern Indiana was preparing himself for a future beyond their wildest dreams (and also beyond his own).

Tom Lincoln seems to have been alternately pleased and provoked by his strange son—who admittedly could be a trial and tribulation to a father trying to get the grubbing, hoeing, and fence making done. Abe could induce every other man and boy in the field to stop working by mounting a stump and going into his act—joking, mimicking, sawing the air with his long arms. At Gentry's store or at the blacksmith shop or at the mill where Lincoln took the corn to be ground, he was soon the favorite entertainer. More often he was to be seen reading books—reading at the table, reading while he plowed, reading by firelight. Tom, who could barely scrawl his name, couldn't see what good could possibly come of so much book reading.

Some say that Lincoln's father was kind to the boy and never tried to interrupt his studying. Dennis Hanks, who felt deeply affectionate toward both Tom and Abe, testified, however, that Tom sometimes beat his son or knocked him "a rod" for being too pert when a stranger came by.

But if the father was stern, Abe's beloved stepmother, Sarah Bush Lincoln, encouraged him in his reading and enjoyed his fun.

Once Lincoln took a small boy with muddy feet, held him upside down, and let him "walk" across the whitewashed ceiling of the cabin. Far from being angry when she saw the footprints, Sarah burst into hilarious laughter. And Abe, who was never malicious in his mischief, quickly mixed a pail of whitewash and covered the muddy tracks. Yes, as Sarah said, their minds seemed harmonious. She never scolded him for reading half the night, nor for bringing a book to his meals. Besides, no one could have stopped young Lincoln from following the magic trail of the printed word into the farthest realms of knowledge.

As Dennis Hanks remembered it, "Seems to me now I never seen Abe after he was twelve 'at he didn't have a book some'ers 'round. He'd put a book inside his shirt an' fill his pants pockets with corn dodgers, an' go off to plow or hoe. When noon came he'd set down under a tree, an' read an' eat. An' when he come to the house at night, he'd tilt a cheer back by the chimbly, put his feet on the rung, an' set on his backbone and read."

Both habits were to remain with Lincoln for life—reading and "sitting on his shoulder blades" while he read. The first books that he devoured were Aesop's Fables, *Robinson Crusoe, Pilgrim's Progress,* and Parson Weems's biography of George Washington. It is probably true as claimed that he studied these books until he had memorized many pages of each. Although it may sound like a myth, there is good evidence that Lincoln did pull corn fodder for two or three days to pay for a borrowed copy of Weems's *Washington* which he had accidentally damaged when rain came through a crack between logs of the cabin, staining the cover of the book.

Many historians have criticized Weems's life of Washington. They particularly scoff at the fable of young Washington cutting the cherry tree with his little hatchet and then confessing the deed to his father because he "could not tell a lie." But little has been said about the powerful and lasting effect of that book on the character of "Honest Abe."

In many respects Lincoln patterned his life on Washington's, and there were interesting similarities between our two most famous presidents.

Both were of English stock; both were tall men (Washington six feet one inch and Lincoln three inches taller); both were athletes in their youth; both learned surveying; and of course both became presidents of the United States. It is also true and significant that both were men of unusual honesty.

In Lincoln's time, all young men were legally bound to their fathers until age twenty-one, and Tom Lincoln never relaxed his claim on his son's labor during all those years. What Abe earned went to his father. Sometimes the boy was "farmed out" to neighbors to butcher pigs at a wage of thirty-one cents a day. Killing a pig is a brutal business. To a boy who had already ceased to hunt because he hated to kill wild animals and who had written essays against cruelty to dumb beasts, slaughtering swine could not have been pleasant work.

One thing about hog butchering that Abe definitely liked, however, was the same thing that he enjoyed about barn raisings, cornhuskings, log rollings, sugar boilings, and all other such neighborhood festivities. It gave him a chance to yarn and joke; to make speeches, race, and wrestle. The fun was rough at frontier frolics. The jokes were often coarse and the drinking heavy. But young Lincoln was considered "game" even though he scarcely touched liquor and used little or no profanity. His fund of knowledge was growing. His stories were amusing and well told by pioneer standards. Abe had a good time at these gatherings.

But his mind had so far outstripped those of most of his neighbors that he now wandered farther and farther from home in search of books or the chance to read a newspaper. His political leanings, which at first favored the Democrats, finally moved toward the Whig point of view. Abe remained a Whig for more than a quarter of a century until he joined the new Republican party in the mid-1850s—the party that finally put him in the White House.

Two books which he discovered at about this time had a powerful and lasting effect on Lincoln's maturing mind. They were the *Revised Laws of Indiana* and *The Columbian Class Book,* both of which he read and reread with the greatest concentration.

The first not only interested Lincoln in the law, which was to become his profession, but reinforced his respect for the Declaration of Independence and its author, Thomas Jefferson. It also excited his interest in several other important documents, such as the first ten amendments to the Constitution. He learned from this volume that in every state of the Old Northwest (Indiana included), slavery must be forever illegal. Thus Lincoln was set to pondering the great theory "that all Men are created equal, that they are endowed by their Creator with certain inalienable Rights, that among these are Life, Liberty and the Pursuit of Happiness."

The second volume, *The Columbian Class Book,* widened his horizons far beyond the United States or even the Western Hemisphere. Here he gained much knowledge about the geography and history of the entire world. This book also explained to Abe that the earth is but one of the several planets revolving around the gigantic, fiery, and distant sun, and that even this sun is but one of the millions of similar suns called stars—those winking lanterns that young Lincoln could see on any clear night in the dark sky above him. Here indeed was a book to expand his horizons.

One evening as the sun was going down in the west and the full moon was arising in the east, Abe sat beside Katy Roby, a neighbor girl, their bare feet dangling in the creek. He told Katy that the sun wasn't really going down or the moon really coming up. What was happening was that the earth was turning like a top on its axis, which made it seem that these heavenly bodies rose or set. Katy and Abe were not in love, they were merely friends. But to the end of her life Katy never forgot that wonderful, simple lesson in astronomy, or how brilliant and knowing Abe Lincoln seemed for all his gangling length and homely appearance as they sat on the bank of the creek on that quiet evening watching the moon rising like a great golden pumpkin through the trees of southern Indiana.

5

Flatboating
Down the Mississippi

I am not ashamed to confess that . . . I was a hired laborer, mauling rails, at work on a flat-boat—just what might happen to any poor man's son!

A. LINCOLN

Throughout his life, Lincoln was interested in boats and in river navigation. Some years before Abe was born, his father, Tom, had built a flat-boat and had taken it, loaded with produce, down the Ohio and the Mississippi to New Orleans. The big rivers of the frontier were the only good highways for carrying such bulky freight as corn and wheat, barrels of pork, and live hogs. And the port of New Orleans was almost the only large market for crops grown in the great valley of the

Mississippi.

Before Abe had his first chance to make a trip downriver, he served a sort of apprenticeship for that adventure. At the age of sixteen, when he was already well over six feet tall, he was hired by James Taylor to build and operate a small ferry-boat at the mouth of Anderson Creek, where that tributary empties into the Ohio. Here he earned thirty-seven cents a day for "the roughest work" a young man could do, and he was sometimes given a few extra coins for rowing passengers to the steamers. On one such occasion when he rushed two anxious men to a waiting riverboat, he was rewarded with two silver half-dollars tossed by the men into his little skiff. He said that he "could scarcely credit that I, a poor boy, had earned a dollar in less than a day."

At seventeen, Lincoln was six feet two inches tall. At nineteen he was a lean, muscular, six-foot-four-inch giant, honest, dependable, droll, and much admired by many of his neighbors—a young man so strong that he could "strike with a maul a heavier blow" than any frontiersman in that part of Indiana. It is little wonder that James Gentry offered him what must have seemed to Abe the opportunity of a lifetime.

Gentry was one of the richest men of the region. He owned the store in Gentryville where Lincoln entertained the idlers with his jokes and tales. He also owned more than one thousand acres of farmland. So when Gentry suggested to Abe that he and Gentry's son Allen build a flatboat and take it to New Orleans, Lincoln leaped at the chance. Abe's job was to work the "foremost oar." He was to be paid eight dollars a month and expenses for the entire time engaged, including the return journey.

Flatboats were among the crudest of all the river vessels. They were made of squared beams and thick planks whipsawed from the limitless supply of timber to be felled anywhere along the Ohio. They ranged from twenty to eighty feet in length and could usually be built for a cost of about one dollar per linear foot. These boats were a combination of "log cabin, fort, floating barnyard, and country grocery" with high enough sides to protect the boatmen against the bullets of marauding Indians and roving river pirates. Heavy, blunt-ended, clumsy to maneuver, and impossible to bring back against the current, they were, however, admirable and inexpensive cargo carriers, able to float a heavy load of grain, whisky, and livestock downstream to the rich port of New Orleans.

Lincoln could not have worried greatly about the difficulty of constructing such a boat. He had helped his father on many minor building projects. He knew the use of adz, axe, drawshave, hammer, plane, and saw. And he had the strength for such heavy labor as felling trees and squaring timbers.

No doubt James Gentry carefully considered all these qualifications in hiring Lincoln. Neither the building of a boat nor the trip down the river was an assignment for a weakling. Life along these broad waterways was rough, tough, and boisterous.

Lincoln was slow to take anger. But James Gentry could be sure that if trouble came on the trip down the river, his son Allen had a good partner to defend the boat and its load of produce. If they could get safely beyond the murderers and brigands of Cave in Rock on the Illinois shore of the

Ohio River, they probably could avoid the lesser nests of pirates and might reach New Orleans in safety.

When the first fiddlehead ferns were curling up through the carpet of the previous year's brown oak leaves, and while the redbud was only a hint of color on dark boughs, Abe and Allen loaded their new boat (still smelling of freshly cut timber) with grain and hogs, bacon and hams, and whatever else James Gentry wished to sell in New Orleans. In April 1828, they cast off from Gentry's Landing to begin their floating adventure down the river.

The wide Ohio flows peacefully here, carrying driftwood downstream. Overhead, in early spring, great flocks of wild ducks and geese fly northward toward their Arctic nesting grounds, the geese uttering the most haunting and desolate cry of any wild fowl on the planet.

Blue kingfishers plunge for their breakfast in every bayou. Turtles sun on the logs. And from a thousand creeks come contributions of water to increase the majestic flow of the big river. From dawn until dark, in sun or rain or fog, Abe and

Allen drifted with the current, tying up at night to sleep under the rude shelter erected at one end of the boat. They safely passed notorious Cave in Rock, and were soon entering the muddy Mississippi.

Ever since 1811 (when Abe had been only two years old), there had been steamboats on the Father of Waters. Eight of these smoke-belching inventions were built for river use in 1817, and there were sixty more within the next two years. So in addition to the arks, sleds, keelboats, barges, and rafts (all loaded with settlers and their household goods and farm implements), Abe and Allen saw a few handsome side-wheelers with their tall smokestacks puffing black clouds into the April sky.

A publication of this era called *The Navigator,* which was the bible of many hundreds of boatmen on western waters, warned of constant dangers. These included high earthen banks of the Mississippi that sometimes collapsed upon craft floating too near the shore, and of "sawyers," "planters," and other timber snags that might pierce the bottom of a boat. "Wooden islands," said the river guide, "are more dangerous than real ones," because the current can pull a vessel under the floating mass of logs and debris.

One night when the flatboat was not far from its final destination, and when it seemed as though the boys would safely reach New Orleans, Abe and Allen tied up at the plantation of a Madame Duchesne.

As Lincoln told it later, "The nature of part of the cargo-load . . . made it necessary . . . to linger and trade along the Sugar coast." And so, on that night as they lay sleeping in their shelter on the boat, they were viciously attacked by seven black bandits who seemed intent on killing and robbing them. They were "hurt some in the melee," but they grabbed hickory clubs and drove off their assailants, chasing them some distance. Then they "cut cable," rowed quickly out into the river, and continued to drift until dawn. Lincoln was wounded above one eye and carried the scar for life. But he did not carry bitterness in his heart, nor draw the false conclusion that all black men were murderers and robbers. He knew that men of all races played the bloody game of river pirate.

Some thirty-five years later Abraham Lincoln would sign the Emancipation Proclamation, foreshadowing the Thirteenth Amendment, which set free every black person in the United States who was enslaved.

The port of New Orleans was a fantastic new world to Abe and Allen, fresh from the woods of southern Indiana. Miles of boats were moored to the wharves. Sailing ships came proudly up the river from the Gulf, with foreign-looking sailors climbing nimbly into the rigging, gold rings dangling from dark ears. The houses of the town were tinted like the rainbow. Over their iron grillwork, flowering vines climbed in fragrant profusion. And in the streets were people of many hues and tongues: Creole, French, Spanish, Mexican. Slaves ranged from creamy tan to ebony. Here were odors, sights, and sounds curious indeed to these young Pigeon Creek frontiersmen. The bells of the cathedral dropped golden notes into the narrow streets, where songs were sung by the revelers and vendors cried their wares.

All too soon their trading was done and it was time to start homeward. The young men took passage on an upriver steamer—probably a luxurious two-decker. The pilot was emperor on this floating kingdom—a fact that put a new idea in young Lincoln's head.

Back in southern Indiana by June, after a two-month round trip, Abe asked his influential friend William Wood if he would do him an important favor.

As Wood later recorded, "Abe came to my house one day and stood round about timid and shy. I knew he wanted something. I said to him, 'Abe, what is your care?' Abe replied, 'Uncle, I want you to go to the River, and give me some recommendation to some boat.' I remarked, 'Abe, your age is against you. You are not 21 yet.' 'I know that, but I want a start,' said Abe."

But for "the boy's good" his friend did not act on his request. And so Lincoln never became a steamboat pilot.

Discontented, sometimes even quarrelsome, reading more avidly than ever, doing what he was asked, but restless, uncertain, and dissatisfied, Abe Lincoln continued to laugh and brood, tell stories and buffoon, perform great feats of physical

51

strength and write crude satires. He seems to have carried on a feud with the Grigsby family, probably because he felt that Aaron Grigsby (who had married his beloved sister Sarah) was somehow responsible for her death through neglect at the birth of her first baby. But he also knew that the time was swiftly arriving when he must become more than his father's chore boy on a poor little half-cleared farm in southern Indiana. He was waiting for his freedom, his twenty-first year, his "start."

And so he could not have been too unhappy when he learned that the family was once again preparing to pull up stakes and move on toward a new frontier—the rich black prairies of central Illinois.

6

The Illinois Frontier

At twenty one I came to Illinois.

A. LINCOLN

Young Abe Lincoln was not the only restless and dissatisfied member of the clan. The milk sickness again had struck along Pigeon Creek, killing in a single week four cows and eleven calves belonging to Dennis Hanks. Thomas Lincoln, still a failure in his fifty-second year, was at least as poor as when he had come to Indiana. He listened hopefully to rumors of fertile new land across the Wabash River in central Illinois.

"Well! Lemme see. Yes; I reckon it was John

53

Hanks 'at got restless fust an' lit out fur Illinois, an' wrote fur us all to come, an' he'd git land fur us," said Dennis Hanks, recalling the reasons why the Lincolns, Hankses, Halls, and Johnstons decided to leave Indiana.

"Tom was always ready to move. He never had his land in Indiany all paid fur, nohow. . . . So he sold off his corn an' hogs an' piled everything into ox-wagons an' we all went—Lincolns an' Hankses an' Johnstons, all hangin' together. I reckon we was like one o' them tribes o' Israel that you kain't break up, nohow. An' Tom was always lookin' fur the land o' Canaan."

The Land of Canaan, the Promised Land of milk and honey on the far side of the Wabash! How frequently "greener pastures" have beckoned to such restless tribes as this one! Tom Lincoln sold his farm for what little it would bring. Farewells were said to friends and neighbors. Soon the wagons, piled high with household goods, women, and children, began their jolting, creaking journey behind the plodding oxen. Abe drove one of the teams, cracking a joke "every time he cracked a whip," or so it seemed to Dennis Hanks.

Often, however, young Lincoln's thoughts must have been on serious matters, such as the great speech which Daniel Webster had just made in the Senate, warning that no state could nullify national law. Lincoln would never forget one ringing line in that speech, "Liberty *and* Union, now and forever, one and inseparable!"

There were thirteen people in this pilgrimage through the icy wilderness: Tom and Sarah Bush Johnston Lincoln and Abraham; Sarah's son, John Johnston; Sarah's daughter Elizabeth, married to Dennis Hanks, and their four children; Sarah's second daughter, Matilda, and her husband, Squire Hall, and their little son. It was a "painfully slow and tiresome" journey, Lincoln later recalled.

The cavalcade moved slowly northward toward Vincennes, the largest town in the state of Indiana. Here they rafted across the Wabash river and began a tedious trek over the Illinois prairies, the wheels of the wagons cutting deep into the half-frozen mud. "It tuk us two weeks to git thar," Dennis Hanks remembered, ". . . cuttin' our way through the woods, fordin' rivers, pryin' wagons an' steers out o' sloughs with fence rails, an' makin' camp."

Streams wandered across these unpopulated wastes. And no bridge had yet been built at any point along the trail. Fording the creeks, the oxen would break through the thin ice at every step. Abe had a little dog who trotted faithfully along beside him all the way. But once when they had just crossed a stream, Lincoln looked back to see the small beast whining pitifully on the far shore, unwilling to brave the plunge into the icy water. "I could not endure the idea of abandoning even a dog," Abe recalled. "Pulling off shoes and socks I waded across the stream and triumphantly returned with the shivering animal under my arm. His frantic leaps of joy and other evidences of a dog's gratitude amply repaid me for all the exposure I had undergone."

On a day early in March 1830, shortly after Lincoln had turned twenty-one, the wagon train reached a bluff "on the North side of the Sangamon river, at the junction of the timberland and prairie, about ten miles Westerly from Decatur."

The five men of the party quickly threw up the

usual cabin. There, crowded in like a family of raccoons in a hollow log, all thirteen of the relatives spent the spring, summer, and autumn of 1830 and almost incredibly savage winter of 1830–31.

Abe had been splitting rails since he was old enough to swing a maul to drive a wedge. However, it was in Illinois that he earned the name of "Rail Splitter," which would later help him to attain the presidency. Young Lincoln not only split most of the rails to fence the ten acres of corn that were planted that first season in Macon County, but with his mother's cousin, John Hanks, he hired out to split some four thousand additional rails for other settlers.

During the spring of 1830 he also cleared and broke virgin prairie soil, holding the big breaking plow to the furrow as it sheared through the heavy roots of brush and bull grass. He was rewarded when the corn came up green and promising—knee-high by the Fourth of July, ripe and full-eared by September. But with autumn came fever and ague to the family. And the winter promised to be severe.

On Christmas Day, 1830, snow began to fall. A bitter wind arose, sweeping the prairie with a blinding blizzard. Many settlers caught even a few hundred yards from their cabins lost their way, floundered, and were frozen to death, their bodies remaining under the enormous drifts until the following spring.

For many days this white fury swirled through the Illinois frontier, obliterating all roads and trails. Soon the snow was three feet deep on the level and rooftop deep in some of the drifts. The thermometer stood at twelve below zero. Then for a brief period rain fell and froze, glazing the drifts with a treacherous coating of ice. Finally the rain ceased and the intense cold returned.

Any horse or cow not under shelter broke through the crust of ice and perished. So did whole herds of white-tailed deer. For a time the wolves feasted on these helpless victims. Then many of the wolves froze to death in their turn. For nine weeks the people in the Lincoln cabin subsisted on little more than cornmeal and melted snow water. They managed to survive. But outside their cabin lay a lifeless and desolate world. Never again would large game return in any quantity to Illinois. It had been obliterated in the "Year of the Deep Snow."

Eventually the warm sun returned and the great drifts began to melt. From the Lincoln cabin, where they had known little but misery and sickness, everyone wished to escape. It was not long before Tom and Sarah moved on to their final home in Coles County. Abe, who had already given his father more months of labor than the law demanded, now felt free to make his own way in the world. What he needed was a job.

An opportunity was offered by Denton Offutt, a dreamer, business plunger, braggart, and heavy drinker, who was willing to hire Lincoln, his stepbrother John Johnston, and John Hanks to take a boatload of produce to New Orleans. Offutt suggested that they join him at Springfield for that purpose when the snow should go off.

"When it did go off," Lincoln remembered, "which was about the 1st. of March 1831—the country was so flooded, as to make traveling by land impracticable." So the young men purchased a large canoe and started down the surging

Sangamon. Thus Lincoln made his "first entrance into Sangamon County."

They found their venturesome businessman at a Springfield tavern. But he did not have the promised flatboat. Abe and the two Johns would have to construct the vessel as well as navigate it if they wished to take a cargo to New Orleans. So they hired themselves to Offutt at twelve dollars per month each, cut timber out of the forest, and built a boat at old Sangamon Town on the Sangamon River. Lincoln seems to have been both boss carpenter and camp cook. The flatboat, which was eighty feet long and eighteen feet wide, was finished in about one month of heavy labor and was soon loaded with corn and barrels of pork. Thirty large and very lively hogs with no desire to take a river journey were brought aboard with the greatest difficulty. All this took time. Meanwhile the flood had receded. So the whole project nearly came to grief on the Rutledge Mill dam at New Salem, where the boat became stranded.

A group of villagers gathered at the river to see the loaded flatboat balancing precariously on the dam. A tall, angular twenty-two-year-old backwoods boy was taking charge of the situation. He wore rolled-up blue jeans, a striped cotton shirt, and a "buckeye chip hat." Wading barefoot, he inspected the boat, which was taking water at the stern, its bow tilted up on the obstruction.

As John Hanks recalled the episode, they "rolled the barrels forward, bored a hole in the end of the boat over the dam—water ran out and thus we got over."

It was Abe Lincoln who worked out the strategy, borrowed the auger to bore the hole, drained the craft, and then plugged the hole and inched the boat over the mill dam. The New Salem villagers watched the young captain of the flatboat with admiration.

Lincoln's cleverness at this moment earned him the further admiration of Denton Offutt, who "conceived a liking for A. and believing he could turn him to account" contracted with him "to act as clerk for him, on his return from New-Orleans," and gave him full charge of a little store in New Salem.

John Johnston, John Hanks, Abe Lincoln, and Denton Offutt proceeded down the winding, snag-choked Sangamon to the Illinois River and from there to the Mississippi. John Hanks turned back at St. Louis while the others continued to New Orleans.

Back home in Illinois after this second trip to New Orleans, Abe made his way to New Salem on the bluff above the dam. The future president of the United States was only too grateful to be wanted as a clerk in a little log-cabin store, in a village of less than a hundred settlers.

7

New Salem and the Black Hawk War

Then I got to New-Salem . . . where I remained . . . as a sort of Clerk in a store. Then came the Black-Hawk war; and I was elected a Captain of Volunteers—a success which gave me more pleasure than any I have had since.

A. LINCOLN

When Abe Lincoln reached New Salem late in July 1831, he considered himself "a piece of floating driftwood." Ignorant of any useful labor except farming, rough carpentry, and flatboating, he was still aimless, untried, and untrained— seemingly without ambition or special talents. When he left that village six years later, prepared for the practice of the law and already locally famous as a successful young legislator, he was on his way toward his great destiny.

The August election was in progress shortly after Lincoln ambled into the bustling little settlement. Abe did not help the schoolmaster, Mentor Graham, record the votes as so many biographers have suggested. But he did vote, probably for the first time. And as the sultry hours dragged slowly by, he also entertained the loungers with jokes and stories such as his tale of the little blue lizard that crawled up the preacher's trouser leg.

This tall, friendly fellow who "could make a cat laugh" but who could also read and write, soon began to make a favorable impression on his new neighbors.

For the next few weeks, while he awaited the stock of goods that Denton Offutt had promised for the store on the bluff above the river, Lincoln spent much of his time getting acquainted with the town and its inhabitants. James Rutledge and John M. Camron had laid out the village two years previously and had built the saw- and grist-mill. Presently there were a dozen cabins flanking the single street, with men, women, and children to fill them to overflowing. Soon this small community could boast a blacksmith, a wheelwright, a bootmaker, a cooper who made barrels, a well-to-do wool merchant, and two doctors who could purge people or set broken bones. William Clary's "grocery" (the frontier term for saloon) attracted at least as many settlers as did the religious services of the Methodists, Baptists, and Cumberland Presbyterians. But it also put youthful rowdies in a mood for interrupting such services.

By the time Denton Offutt reached New Salem with his merchandise, his storekeeper was already popular with many of the villagers. But he had yet to impress himself upon the Clary's Grove boys—the hard-riding, hard-drinking, hard-fighting coterie of tough young men who came to town each Saturday whooping like Indians and ready for a riot. The Clary grocery, only thirty steps from the Offutt store, was the New Salem headquarters of this gang of revelers who competed endlessly by racing on horseback or afoot, broadjumping, throwing the maul, and wrestling and fighting for the sheer joy of battle.

Offutt was a boastful little man who could not

have lasted two minutes in a brawl with one of the Clary's Grove boys. But he soon began bragging that his clerk, Abe Lincoln, could whip any one of them in a wrestling match. He was willing to bet five dollars on Abe, and he found a taker for his bet.

Jack Armstrong, champion of the Grove and of the grocery, was known as the best fighter and wrestler in twenty miles. When New Salem learned that the powerful newcomer, Abe Lincoln, and the unbeaten Jack Armstrong were scheduled for a match, bets ranged from drinks and jackknives to actual money as the excited crowd gathered.

The famous fight, which was to have far-reaching political consequences for Lincoln, happened on a Saturday afternoon. Within the circle of tense onlookers, Jack and Abe, stripped to the waist, circled warily, seeking an opening. Jack was shorter than Abe, but built like a young bull. His heavy biceps and shoulders gleamed and rippled in the sunlight. Abe's long, flat muscles had gigantic strength and leverage, but he knew that he was facing a tough opponent.

Stories of how the match ended differ in a few respects. But most versions agree that after a rough struggle, Abe threw Jack fairly. Then the rest of the Clary's Grove gang jumped Abe, who sprang to his feet, placed his back to a wall, and offered to take on the entire crowd, but one at a time. Armstrong, like the good sport he ever after proved to be, pushed aside his companions and offered Lincoln his hand. He and his wife, Hannah, were to remain friends of Lincoln for life, strong supporters in every political campaign. And Lincoln, in his turn, was able to do the Armstrongs favors they would never forget.

When Lincoln had also proved that he could out-run, out-jump, and throw the maul farther than any brawny man in the community, his growing leadership was quickly accepted. And this was true despite the fact that evidently he did not drink, gamble, or brag of his prowess.

If the frontier admired brawn, it also admired brains. The half-dozen well-educated men in the town began to see in Lincoln other virtues than his physical strength. The schoolteacher, Mentor

Graham, gladly helped Lincoln with his grammar and mathematics. Jack Kelso, who would rather have fished and quoted poetry than labored for a living, was soon interesting Abe in the plays of Shakespeare and the poetry of Robert Burns. The local literary and debating society gave Lincoln his first chance to make a serious and reasoned speech. Such men as James Rutledge and Dr. Francis Regnier were amazed at Abe's lucid oratory. They realized that all young Lincoln needed was practice and polish to make him a forceful speaker.

In only one respect did Abe seem to be deficient. At Offutt's store and on later occasions, he proved to be a poor businessman. People liked him for his friendliness and his absolute honesty. But Lincoln was far more interested in reading books and telling stories than in selling calico, salt, sugar, tea, and other merchandise.

Very soon Offutt tired of the store and left town for other business ventures, so Abe was out of a steady job by spring. But that seven-month period in New Salem, with its widening circle of friendship, must have given Lincoln confidence, because on March 9, 1832, he announced that in the forthcoming election he would run for the state legislature.

With the help of Mentor Graham and others, Abe wrote his first political platform. It might have been briefer. But it scarcely could have been more shrewdly designed to capture Sangamon County votes.

Frankly a supporter of Henry Clay, as opposed to the popular Andrew Jackson, Lincoln based his appeal almost entirely on local issues: a decrease in interest rates on loans (most of the voters were in debt); an improvement in educational opportunities (there were virtually no schools); and finally, an improvement in transportation by straightening the Sangamon River. He believed that vessels of "25 to 30 tons burthen" could come up the Sangamon as far as the South Fork. He made the interesting suggestion that the river could wash its own deep, straight channel if workmen were to cut through the bends and oxbows. And he concluded his first campaign document with a paragraph almost certain to gain him sympathy:

I was born and have ever remained in the most humble walks of life. . . . if the good people in their wisdom shall see fit to keep me in the background, I have been too familiar with disappointments to be very much chagrined. Your friend and fellow-citizen.

A. LINCOLN

At about this time, New Salem and surrounding villages were thrown into a frenzy of excitement by the announcement that a little steamboat named the *Talisman,* under the charter of Captain Vincent Bogue, would "deliver freight from St. Louis" at the landing on the Sangamon River, six miles north of the town of Springfield, "for thirty-seven-and-a-half cents per 100 pounds!" This was about half what it cost to freight merchandise overland. Farmers and merchants could visualize quick prosperity if goods and produce could be so cheaply shipped to and from the Illinois frontier.

It was Abe Lincoln, candidate for the legislature, who led the crew of men armed with poles, cant hooks, and long-handled axes that preceded the boat up the winding Sangamon, clearing away snags and overhanging branches. Among the citizens on horseback cheering this progression was a thirteen-year-old boy, Billy Herndon, who was later to become Lincoln's third law partner, his biographer, and hero worshiper. Herndon never forgot Abe's leadership of the axmen, cutting that passage for the *Talisman*.

After a riotous welcome the steamboat unloaded its cargo and started back downstream. But the river was no longer flooded. Lincoln, copilot of the vessel on its downstream journey, managed the return trip, but only with the greatest difficulty.

The excitement surrounding the arrival of the *Talisman* had barely subsided when a new sensation—this time of fear and horror—swept the countryside.

Black Hawk, the venerable war chief of the Sac and Fox tribes, was gathering his forces. Nearly four hundred well-armed Indians were on the warpath. Having crossed the Mississippi, they were threatening to drive white settlers from ancient Indian corn fields and village sites in Illinois and Wisconsin.

This brave old leader of his tribe wanted to regain the rich land from which his people had so long taken their grain. "My reason teaches me," Black Hawk argued, "that land cannot be sold. The Great Spirit gave it to his children to live upon. So long as they occupy and cultivate it they have the right to the soil. Nothing can be sold but such things as can be carried away."

But whatever the justice of his claim, Black Hawk had signed a treaty which he was now violating. His warriors were striking terror among the settlers, who were being shot, tomahawked, and scalped. From the isolated settlements in northern Illinois came swift messengers begging for armed assistance. A call was sent out by the governor of Illinois, and the volunteers assembled rapidly. Lincoln, through popular vote, was elected captain of his company, largely through the influence of the Clary's Grove boys, who were now his most ardent admirers. As was only proper, Jack Armstrong became Abe's first sergeant.

Many humorous stories were told by Lincoln and others about the unmilitary nature of his command. His raw recruits were boisterous, unshaven, and difficult to discipline. Abe held them in line principally by offering to fight any man who disobeyed him. But Lincoln knew so little about drill-field terminology that once, as his company approached a narrow gate twenty abreast, he could think of no command to turn them "endwise." So he shouted the following order: "Halt! This company will break ranks for two minutes and form again on the other side of the gate."

Lincoln and his company never saw Black Hawk's warriors, nor heard a gun fired in battle. But once Abe saved the life of an old Indian who, although he came into camp with a pass, stood in danger of being murdered by the soldiers. And once he and his company helped to bury five militiamen who had been killed in an earlier engagement at Kellogg's Grove. Lincoln would never forget the way those dead men looked with the "red light of the morning sun" streaming over them as they lay on the ground. "And every man had a round, red spot on top of his head . . . where the redskins had taken his scalp. It was frightful, but it was grotesque and the red sunlight seemed to paint everything all over. I re-member that one man had on buckskin breeches."

Meanwhile old Black Hawk had been tricked, defeated, and captured. Taken to Washington, D.C., he stood straight and proud before President Andrew Jackson and said, "I—am—a man—and you—are—another . . . I took up the hatchet . . . to revenge injuries which my people could no longer endure. Had I borne them longer . . . my people would have said, 'Black Hawk . . . is too old to be a chief; he is no Sac.' "

Lincoln was mustered out in southern Wiscon-sin. Since his horse had been stolen, it was neces-sary to make his way home to New Salem on foot and by canoe.

Years later in a speech he made in Congress deriding Lewis Cass, Democratic candidate for the presidency, Abe was satirical concerning the mil-itary record of both himself and General Cass:

"By the way, Mr. Speaker, did you know I am a military hero? Yes sir; in the days of the Black Hawk war, I fought, bled, and came away. Speak-ing of General Cass's career reminds me of my own. . . . It is quite certain I did not break my sword, for I had none to break; but I bent a musket pretty badly on one occasion. . . . If General Cass went in advance of me in picking huckleberries, I guess I surpassed him in charges upon the wild onions. If he saw any live, fighting Indians, it was more than I did."

Back home in New Salem, however, Lincoln found that brief service for his country appeared to be no liability in his campaign for election to the state legislature. With little time left to promote his candidacy, Abe went about the countryside talking to farmers, helping with the harvesting of grain, making occasional speeches. At Pappsville, where he spoke at a cattle auction, he found it necessary briefly to interrupt his address while he tossed a bully out of the crowd. Casually he returned to the stump. He wore on this occasion a "mixed jeans coat" with claw-hammer tails too short to sit on, tow-linen pantaloons much too short, and a straw hat with no band. His speech was a model of brevity, which all politicians might profitably study:

"Fellow Citizens, I presume you all know who I am—I am humble Abraham Lincoln. I have been solicited by many friends to become a candidate for the legislature. My politics are short and sweet, like the old woman's dance. I am in favor of a national bank. I am in favor of the internal improvement system and a high protective tariff. These are my sentiments and political principles. If elected I shall be thankful; if not, it will be all the same."

Lincoln lost the election, for the only time in his life "on the direct vote of the people." But he won his own precinct "277 for and 7 against." He was easily the most popular man in New Salem, and he had been elected captain of his company. Humble Abe Lincoln had tributes of affection and evidences of public approval to warm the cockles of his heart in that late summer of 1832.

8

Jack of All Trades

The store winked out.

A. LINCOLN

During the next five years, Lincoln was a store-keeper, postmaster, surveyor, state assemblyman, and newly licensed lawyer. In all of these ventures except the first he was successful. His business dealings in connection with the store were so unfortunate that, although he was penniless when he began, he was actually about a thousand dollars in debt when he left New Salem for Springfield in 1837.

Why the desire to be a merchant? Abe probably

remembered the honorable position in the community held by the storekeeper James Gentry back in Indiana. Doubtless, too, he enjoyed the continual contacts across the counter with his neighbors and the chance it gave him to tell stories. Above all else, here was an opportunity to rise above manual labor, leisure to lie on the counter with his feet propped on the wall high above his head, reading every book on which he could lay his big, gnarled, work-hardened hands.

In later years Lincoln recalled that he was eager to remain in New Salem among friends who had treated him with "so much generosity." For a time he thought of "learning the blacksmith trade— thought of trying to study law." But he decided he could not succeed at that without a better education.

Out of work, and in need of keeping body and soul together, he was amazed when "a man offered to sell and did sell," to Lincoln and to another as poor as himself, "an old stock of goods, upon credit." They opened as merchants, but they did nothing but get deeper and deeper in debt.

The story of the store that "winked out" has

been told so many times that it seems almost legendary—but the tale is true. Lincoln and his partner, William F. Berry, soon proved an unlikely pair of merchants. Berry drank deep from the whisky barrel. Lincoln drank deep from his books. Together they managed to destroy the business in a matter of months. But it was Honest Abe—the man who would walk miles to return an accidental overcharge of a few cents—who was left with all the debts when the store failed. After many years of labor he paid those debts to the last penny.

To meet his board bill at the Rutledge tavern, Lincoln was willing to take any sort of casual labor—splitting rails, husking corn, or clerking at the new store run by A. Y. Ellis. On May 7, 1833, he was appointed postmaster of New Salem, a part-time job that paid him perhaps fifty to seventy-five dollars a year, but that also allowed him the privilege of reading all the newspapers mailed to subscribers in the village.

Back in Indiana, Abe had been known as "a sort of newsboy," reciting in summary all the news he could remember from the papers that he read so avidly. Eager for information about the world, national affairs, and political issues, Lincoln continued to devour the contents of such newspapers as the St. Louis *Missouri Republican,* the *Louisville Journal,* the Washington *National Intelligencer,* and the Springfield *Sangamo Journal.* In New Salem he was often to be seen in the center of a group of loungers reading aloud some paper not yet claimed at the post office.

Another pleasure for Lincoln, if he was going that way and in the mood, was to deliver letters. He carried them in his hat, a catchall that over the years would also accommodate legal notes and documents, correspondence of all sorts, in fact anything the hat's owner might need at a moment's notice. Abe had to be careful when he tipped his hat to a lady that he didn't spill a bushel of paper.

Obviously young Abraham Lincoln was not storing up money in New Salem, but he was storing up other riches—those of the mind: grammar, mathematics, and, before long, the elements of surveying and the principles of the law.

One might almost believe that the village of New Salem was created by magic for the single purpose of helping Abraham Lincoln to evolve into the man he later became. Founded only two years before Lincoln's arrival, this little town virtually disappeared from the map two years after Abe's departure. It was as though at the wave of some sorcerer's wand, log cabins had appeared on the bluff above the Sangamon; as though at another wave of the wand a cast of characters was summoned out of thin air.

But while they lived in their New Salem cabins, these characters in the Lincoln drama were very real indeed, and often played an important role in Abe's development. For instance, it was Sangamon County Surveyor John Calhoun of Springfield who offered Lincoln a job as his assistant in establishing the boundaries of farms, laying out towns, and surveying new roads. Abe knew nothing of this profession, so he went to live with the schoolteacher, Mentor Graham, who sat up with Lincoln every night explaining Flint's *System of Geometry . . . with Treatise on Surveying* and Gibson's *A Treatise of Practical Surveying*. Graham's wife, Sarah, complained that her husband and Lincoln, talking beside the fire, kept her

81

awake until hours after midnight.

Many years later Graham was to say that during his long career as a teacher he had never discovered anyone who learned as readily as Lincoln, the "most studious, diligent, strait forward young man in the pursuit of knowledge and literature than any among the five thousand I have taught in schools."

Soon Lincoln, with compass and chain, was crashing through the sumac, hazel brush, and poison ivy, stamping through the bull grass, scaling the wooded bluffs, and wading the marshes as he laid out farms, roads, and villages of central Illinois. He was paid $2.50 for establishing a quarter section (one hundred sixty acres), plus two dollars a day expenses. But he was not always paid in cash. For one of his first jobs he was rewarded with two "bucks"—literally buckskins, which Hannah Armstrong, wife of Jack, "foxed" onto his pantaloons to keep them from being ripped by thorns and briers.

None of these jobs, nor all of them together, could support Lincoln and also pay his debts. To add to his miseries, men to whom he owed money forced the seizure of his horse, saddle, bridle, and surveying instruments, which were then sold at public auction. Luckily a friend bought these possessions and returned them to Abe, as proof of his faith in the struggling young surveyor.

Early in 1834 Lincoln decided once again to run for the state legislature. With the support of both the Democrats and the Whigs, he was elected. Bowling Green, the rotund justice of the peace, was his Democratic supporter. John T. Stuart, a prominent Springfield lawyer and himself a Whig candidate for the General Assembly, managed the strategy in Lincoln's own party. Stuart also became Lincoln's sponsor in other important ways, guiding him along the difficult paths of state politics when the Assembly met in Vandalia the following December, urging Lincoln to read law, lending him the needed books, and eventually taking Abe in as a law partner a few years later.

So now, in addition to all his other studies, Lincoln was reading Blackstone's *Commentaries* and Chitty's *Pleadings,* attempting to master both of these classic foundations of a legal training.

Abe continued to survey and accept odd jobs

far into the autumn of 1834. Then, borrowing two hundred dollars from his friend Coleman Smoot, he bought his first tailor-made suit of clothes for sixty dollars and prepared to make his appearance in the lower house of the General Assembly at Vandalia, then the capital of Illinois.

Roads were muddy in those days, particularly in late November. When the mud-splattered stagecoach rolled into the straggling prairie village of Vandalia on the unfinished Cumberland Road, there was little of interest to see except the two-story brick capitol building, and the legislators and their families arriving for the current session of the Assembly. But to Lincoln, following Stuart into the tavern where they intended to stay, this town of six hundred people was a place of glittering opportunity.

It would be somewhat fruitless to follow this new state legislator from Sangamon County through all four of the two-year terms that he served in the Illinois Assembly. It is true that Abe was learning the primary problems of politics in a rough school. But an unsympathetic observer might have said that his progress was merely from splitting logs to "rolling" them. A "logroller" in politics is a person who returns one favor for another. He votes for a bill another politician wants passed and that politician agrees to do him a similar favor. Unfortunately, today, as in the era of Lincoln, politicians make many such compromises.

During his eight years in the legislature, Lincoln rose to the position of "minority leader," a power in the politics of his state. He was often able to bring great pressure to bear on other assemblymen when he wished to push through a piece of legislation.

Illinois, like many other states at that time, had gone quite insane over internal improvements. It is true that roads, canals, and railroads were desperately needed by the entire frontier. But in a year when the balance in the Illinois state treasury was about two thousand dollars, it seems to have been utter madness to have voted canals and other transportation projects costing millions.

During Lincoln's third year in office, he used all of his shrewd political power to capitalize on this eagerness for new roads, canals, and railroads that were demanded by every county in Illinois. As leader of the "Long Nine" from Sangamon County (seven legislators and two state senators, all averaging over six feet tall), Lincoln, the tallest of the group, utilized the combined length and strength of these big men virtually to dominate the Assembly.

The Democrats wanted the new transportation systems. Lincoln and his friends wanted the state capital to be moved from Vandalia to Springfield. Tremendous logrolling brought the desired results. The roads, canals, and railroads were voted. So was the change in the site of the capital. Springfield celebrated its great victory over Vandalia. And Lincoln, who had done much to aid the Springfield cause, was hailed there as something of a hero.

It was while still in Vandalia that Lincoln first came to know two men who were later to become his opponents. One was James Shields, who would one day challenge Lincoln to a duel. The other was the stocky, pugnacious, brilliant, but not wholly admirable Stephen A. Douglas, whom Lincoln would face in a series of famous debates in the late 1850s that were to echo across the entire nation. At a big dinner given at one of the taverns, Lincoln watched Shields and Douglas waltz the length of the long table to the huzzahs of celebrating politicians. The next day Shields paid six hundred dollars for broken dishes and glassware at a moment in our history when that much money would have purchased a large and fertile farm.

If Lincoln played "practical" politics, it is not to be thought that he did not also cling to many of his dreams and ideals. With internal improvements and the relocation of the state capital out of the way, Lincoln found occasion to express publicly his views on slavery—views that changed little in the next twenty-four years. He let it be known to the Assembly that he felt slavery was founded on injustice and bad policy, but that he was no abolitionist. He did not feel that the federal government had the right to interfere with slavery in those states where it was already established, but he did feel that Congress could abolish it in the District of Columbia.

Thus, even as a young man, Lincoln was beginning to express his conviction that the evil of slavery must never be allowed to spread.

Back home in New Salem, where Lincoln spent the months between sessions of the state legislature, there lived a girl named Ann Rutledge, the blue-eyed, auburn-haired daughter of James Rutledge. Ann and Lincoln became good friends.

But did Lincoln ever propose to Ann? Did she accept him? And was her death in 1835 such a crushing blow to Lincoln that for a time he nearly lost his reason?

Modern biographers doubt there really was a tragic love affair. It appears that William Herndon, who later became Lincoln's law partner and biographer, was responsible for the romantic myth that was so widely accepted until recent years.

Whatever the facts, New Salem in time began to lose its charm for Abraham Lincoln. In April 1837, when Abe was twenty-eight (with just twenty-eight more years to live), he moved to Springfield to begin his practice of the law.

Behind him he left many memories—of a store that had "winked out"; of a postmastership that allowed him to read the always fascinating newspapers; of rail splitting, cornhusking, and surveying. Of good talks by firelight with his many friends. Of books he had read. Of votes his neighbors had always given him when he ran for office. And of a girl he had known who now lay beneath the prairie sod. Yet within another two years New Salem would become a ghost village.

9

Early Days in Springfield

I had studied law, and removed to Springfield to practice it.

A. LINCOLN

Joshua F. Speed, a young, handsome, and prosperous Kentucky-bred merchant who was soon to become Lincoln's best friend, recalled Abe's humble arrival in Springfield, where the future president was to live for the next twenty-four years. He came on a borrowed horse with all of his possessions in two saddlebags. Entering Speed's store, Lincoln asked "what the furniture for a single bedstead would cost"; and when Speed calculated it would come to seventeen dollars, Lincoln said it was probably cheap enough, but added that "cheap as it is, I have not the money to pay. But if you will credit me until Christmas, and my experiment here as a lawyer is a success, I will pay you then. If I fail in that I will probably never pay you at all."

Looking at the tall, ungainly man whose face was remembered by many as the saddest they had ever seen, Speed made a quick decision. He said to the melancholy young lawyer leaning on his counter:

"As so small a debt seems to affect you so deeply, I think I can suggest a plan by which you will be able to attain your end without incurring any debt. I have a very large room which you are perfectly welcome to share with me if you choose."

"Where is the room?" Lincoln asked.

"Upstairs," Speed answered, indicating a stairway leading to the floor above. Picking up his saddlebags, Lincoln mounted the stairs two at a time. When he came down again he was smiling with relief. He had decided to move in.

Although in a letter written soon after his arrival Lincoln complained of his loneliness, he was in many ways a fortunate man. Joshua Speed's generosity gave him not only a rent-free home but a club and forum as well. In a big room at the back of the store, heated with a fireplace, several of the bright young men of the town gathered frequently to discuss literature and argue politics. Speed, who was probably as well-read as Lincoln and considerably more polished, and Speed's bright and dapper clerk Billy Herndon were two of the regulars. Sometimes they were joined by the successful young politician Stephen A. Douglas, who was as short, aggressive, and Democratic as Lincoln was tall, conciliatory, and Whig. Often these men and others would merely joke, tell anecdotes, and quote poetry far into the night. At other times Lincoln and Douglas would square off in a serious political argument—a well-matched pair of debaters.

In other ways, too, Lincoln was fortunate. It was at this time that John T. Stuart, who had encouraged him to study law, took Lincoln as his partner. And although the Stuart–Lincoln account book shows that the usual legal fee charged by this firm during their first year was a mere five dollars, at least the partnership was a respected and going concern.

Furthermore, young Lincoln was already popular in Springfield for having shrewdly planned the political strategy that shifted the Illinois state capital from Vandalia to its new site.

Because a state census had been taken two years previous, it is easy to picture this town of fifteen hundred citizens at the time of Lincoln's arrival. There were exactly as many retail groceries (saloons, that is) as there were churches: six of each. The inhabitants of this sprawling community could buy dry goods at nineteen separate establishments. There were four hotels, four drugstores, and four coffeehouses. There were two rival newspapers that eventually became almost the personal mouthpieces of those lifelong political rivals, Abraham Lincoln and Stephen A. Douglas. Lincoln's loyal supporter Simeon Francis edited the *Sangamo Journal*. Douglas, on the other hand, could count on the friendship and editorial support of the *Illinois Republican* (later the *Illinois State Register*), edited by George R. Weber.

Most of the stores and offices faced the central

square or were to be found on adjoining downtown streets. Farther out lay a crazy quilt of habitations, mingling log cabins with substantial residences of frame or brick.

But throughout this overgrown village, the streets were unpaved—clouds of dust in dry weather and quagmires of deep, black Illinois mud when it rained. Pigs wallowed at random even on the square, and crossing a street was sometimes a sporting event. Many aspects of life in the new state capital were rough and ready, raw and unrefined.

By way of contrast, both the young city and the young lawyer had intellectual interests too. Springfield could boast a bookstore, an academy, and several private schools. It also had a Thespian Society, a Temperance Society, and the Young Men's Lyceum. Famous personalities like Daniel Webster came to lecture. Few American towns of fifteen hundred people today could display a more lively concern with books and ideas than frontier Springfield. And few citizens in that pioneer community took a greater interest in cultural matters than Abraham Lincoln.

The hospitality of Springfield was warm and generous. Ninian W. Edwards and his wife, Elizabeth Todd Edwards, were among the social leaders of a fashionable set made up largely of Kentuckians. To this circle Lincoln was readily admitted. As the law partner of John T. Stuart and the leader of the Whigs in the State Assembly, he was an asset to any gathering even if he did dress carelessly, speak with a backwoods accent, and monopolize the attention of guffawing male listeners who should have been asking the young ladies to dance.

Tradition insists that it was at a cotillion ball connected with the first session of the legislature to be held in Springfield that Lincoln met Mary Todd, the small, plump, blue-eyed, witty, well-educated, temperamental younger sister of Mrs. Edwards. It has been said that the candle-lit room was decorated with flowers, and that no girl at the cotillion was more attractive than little Mary Todd in her low-cut ball gown.

Tall, gawky Abraham Lincoln in his ill-fitting black could not keep his mind on his droll stories, or his eyes from the pretty girl who danced now with Stephen Douglas, now with James Shields or some other young admirer. Finally, screwing up his courage, he approached the sparkling Miss Todd and confided that he wanted to dance with her in "the worst way." As Mary Todd later remembered it, "He certainly did."

Thus began one of the most stormy courtships leading to one of the most perplexing marriages in American history.

No two people could have been more dissimilar than Abraham and Mary. Lincoln had been permitted less than one year of rudimentary frontier schooling. Mary Todd was the product of two private academies where she had studied French, drama, dancing, music, literature, and the social graces. Not only was Lincoln's parentage humble, but he himself sometimes felt that on the Hanks side it was faintly disreputable. The Todds, on the other hand, were one of the more important families in Kentucky. Lincoln was easygoing, modest, generous-minded, tolerant, and forgiving. Mary was neat, prim, fussy, extravagant, vain, often unforgiving, and frequently subject to extreme temper tantrums. Lincoln was only moderately ambitious. Mary was one of the most ambitious women Springfield had ever seen.

At a time when she was being squired around by Lincoln, Douglas, and James Shields, Mary was sometimes asked which man she hoped to marry. More than once she answered that she would choose the one most likely to become president. In Lincoln and Douglas she had two remarkably well-matched contenders. Perhaps with her driving ambition, Mary could have made a president of either one of them.

And yet no such unflattering portrait of Mary Todd gives the whole picture. Mary Todd also had charm and vivacity and intelligence. Certainly she held Lincoln spellbound when not driving him to the depths of his chronic melancholia. Together they talked literature and politics—two interests they held in common. According to Mary's sister, when Lincoln visited, it was Mary who usually set the pace of the conversation. "Mr. Lincoln would sit at her side and listen. He scarcely said a word, but gazed on her as if irresistibly drawn toward her by some superior and unseen power."

During that first year after they met, the courtship appeared to be progressing as well as such a curious romance could. Sometime in 1840 they became engaged, despite objections from the Edwards household that Lincoln was not a suitable husband. What happened soon thereafter is still disputed by Lincoln's biographers. With the coming of winter something chilled in Lincoln's troubled heart. On January 1, 1841, the engagement was broken by Lincoln, whose reasons are still obscure.

Then came nearly two years of misery for both of them, particularly for Lincoln, whose despair was so deep that for days he would not leave his room. As during a previous brief love affair with a young woman named Mary Owens, who had rejected his proposal of marriage, Lincoln found himself depressed, unsure of himself, and unable to make decisions.

It is believed that Lincoln's trip to Kentucky to visit Joshua Speed helped to restore his mental health and happiness. Speed, who had returned to his native state, was engaged to a beautiful girl named Fanny Henning, but was almost as reluctant as Lincoln to go through with the wedding.

It would seem that Lincoln, in trying to convince Speed that such reluctance was absurd, also convinced himself. And when Speed wrote of his married happiness, the letter gave Lincoln "more pleasure, than the total sum of all I have enjoyed since that fatal first of Jany. '41."

It was probably the wife of Simeon Francis, editor of the *Sangamo Journal*, who brought Lincoln and Mary Todd together again. She let them use her house as a secret rendezvous. And it was doubtless here that these two conspirators gaily collaborated on the "Lost Township" letters which might well have cost Lincoln his life.

Since his middle teens Abe had been addicted to writing stinging satire for purposes of humor. Now he put this talent to use in his political feuding. Since he had free access to the columns of the *Sangamo Journal*, he found the temptation irresistible to write witty attacks on some of his enemies, signing his articles with pen names. One of these was "Sampson's Ghost."

Now Lincoln and Mary, possibly with the aid of Mary's closest friend, Julia Jayne, dreamed up a new fictitious letter writer to the *Sangamo Journal*, a farm woman from the "Lost Townships" who signed herself "Aunt Becca." Her tongue was remarkably tart and salty and her victim was none other than Lincoln's rival in politics (and, briefly, in love), the Irish-born state auditor James Shields.

Lincoln, who with his fellow Whigs had helped to drive the state deep into debt, took obviously unfair advantage of Shields in blaming him and his party for a situation in state finances which was more Lincoln's fault than Shields's.

The whole plot assumes a slightly disgraceful aspect. But Lincoln would never have found himself facing the challenge to apologize or fight had it not been for a final and far more insulting letter written in Lincoln's absence by Mary Todd and Julia Jayne and again signed "Aunt Becca." It could hardly have been more effective in calling forth a challenge. Aunt Becca proclaimed that if Shields insisted on fighting, she wanted fair play. Shields could wear a petticoat, or she would put on breeches.

Badgered beyond endurance, Shields insisted that the editor reveal the real author of the attacks. Lincoln, taking responsibility for all the letters, tried to straighten out the mess without a complete public apology. Unsuccessful in this, he reluctantly accepted Shields' challenge and named as weapons the largest cavalry sabers. Shields had once been a fencing instructor, so Lincoln's choice of weapons would have seemed suicidal were it not for the second stipulation, which made the whole matter wildly ludicrous. According to Lincoln's terms of acceptance, the duelists would not be allowed to step across a plank set in the earth between them, nor could they step farther back from the plank than the length of the sword plus three feet. Thus Lincoln, without dishonor, could retreat the allotted distance and not commit an undesired murder, and Shields, for all his superior knowledge of fencing, would be utterly unable to reach Lincoln without stepping across the plank. The seconds, who were far more violent than the principals, continued to fan the flames of anger. But when they met at the appointed hour on the Missouri shore of the Mississippi across from Alton, Illinois, all differences were settled without a fight.

There were, however, at least two interesting

postscripts to this near duel. Lincoln never again attacked opponents with anonymous letters. And Mary Todd, doubtless touched deeply and romantically by Lincoln's chivalrous gesture in her defense, soon agreed to a quick marriage.

Only a few close friends were present when the two plighted their troth "till death do us part" on November 4, 1842, in the home of Elizabeth and Ninian Edwards. And so, "for better, for worse; for richer, for poorer; in sickness and in health" they were joined together for their long uphill struggle toward Mary's great ambition—a term in the White House, with Abraham president and Mary the first lady of the land.

10

Congressman and Lawyer

*In 1846 I was once elected to the lower House of
Congress.*

A. LINCOLN

During his professional lifetime, Lincoln had three
law partners: first John T. Stuart, who has been
mentioned, then Stephen T. Logan, and finally
William H. Herndon. When Stuart and Lincoln
dissolved their partnership in 1841, Lincoln became associated with Logan. One of the most astute legal brains in Illinois, he was a thin little man
with a great mop of red hair, who was as casual
about his appearance as Lincoln himself, but who
prepared his cases far more carefully. Logan taught

his rather slipshod partner to make better use of his law books and to prepare his cases with order and precision. This made Lincoln a more effective attorney than he had been in the past, although Logan was later to describe him somewhat slightingly as "a pretty good lawyer" whose general knowledge of the law "was never formidable."

In 1844 Logan decided that he preferred his own son as a partner. Lincoln, now without an associate, surprised twenty-six-year-old Billy Herndon by offering him a partnership. "I was young in the practice," Herndon remembered, "and was painfully aware of my want of ability and experience; but when he remarked in his earnest, honest way, 'Billy, I can trust you, if you can trust me,' I felt relieved, and accepted the generous proposal."

Lincoln's offer *was* generous. But it was not as careless and uncalculating as it might appear. Herndon had political influence with the "shrewd wild boys" about town, who were an important element in the outcome of any election. His formal education was better than Lincoln's and he had a wider grasp of several subjects, particularly philosophy. It is probable that by this time Lincoln preferred to be the senior partner for a change. And in selecting Billy Herndon for the junior role, he chose a young man whose respect for "Mr. Lincoln" gradually became hero worship, mingled, however, with a growing trace of subconscious envy.

In contrast to Lincoln's rumpled, ill-fitting clothes, Herndon was something of a dandy, sporting patent-leather shoes and neat kid gloves. Both men wore tall silk hats with narrow brims, but Herndon's was shining and spotless, while Lincoln's rusty stovepipe was usually stoked with legal papers.

To the time of Lincoln's death, this oddly matched pair were congenial co-workers with never a written word to legalize their partnership. They split their fees equally and casually—fifty-fifty. And although Herndon and Lincoln's wife, Mary, were anything but friendly, this smoldering feud appears never to have come between "Billy" and "Mr. Lincoln," as they always called each other.

Lincoln was fortunate in having such an amiable law partner because his life at home was not always pleasant. As the few existing letters and several telegrams between them seem to show, Mary and Abraham genuinely loved each other. They shared their tragedies and triumphs together, entertained successfully, and pulled as a well-matched team during hard-fought political campaigns. Each had a mind worthy of the other's.

But Mary's headaches, temper tantrums, and biting tongue often made their home life less than tranquil. She was frequently unsparing in her criticism of her husband's easygoing ways, his frontier manners, broad humor, and eccentric habit of reading while lying on the floor with his feet above his head. However, Mary had her eccentricities too. She was so terrified during any thunderstorm that at the first distant rumble from the cloudy sky Lincoln would hurry home to comfort his distraught wife.

When they were first married they lived at the Globe tavern in Springfield, paying four dollars a week for room and board. It was here that their first child, Robert Todd Lincoln, was born in August 1843. The following January, they purchased for fifteen hundred dollars a cottage, which with a later enlargement was to house them comfortably until they moved to the White House in Washington in 1861. It was in their Springfield home that three more boys were born to the pair: Edward Baker, called Eddy, who arrived in 1846; William Wallace, answering to Willie, who came in 1850; and Thomas, affectionately known as Tad, who was their last child, arriving in 1853. Of the four, only Robert Todd Lincoln grew to manhood.

Love for these children, fear for their health, and long vigils spent at their bedsides when they were ill brought Abraham and Mary closer together. But this doting father and mother found it difficult ever to discipline their sons. Billy Herndon, who was never quite fair in his judgment of anyone Lincoln loved, called the boys "brats." They drove Billy wild when Lincoln brought them to the office on Sunday mornings.

While their father read aloud to himself, entirely unaware of their mischief, these young rascals "soon gutted the room—gutted the shelves of books—rifled the drawers and riddled boxes—battered the points . . . of gold pens against the stove—turned over the ink stands on the papers—scattered letters over the office and danced over them." What Herndon felt that they needed was a good, sound spanking. But Lincoln, who loved to romp with them and share their games, was no more inclined than Mary to correct systematically their bad manners. It is probable that Lincoln, who had frequently been "knocked a rod" by his angry father, and whose own youth had been bitterly hard, thus overcompensated by being too lenient with his own children.

Always, however, he was a man who was tolerant and affectionate with children, as many anecdotes prove. Lincoln was six feet four inches tall. His silk hat towered skyward several additional inches. So a string tightly stretched between trees about seven feet above the sidewalk would let everyone else pass untouched but would knock off Lincoln's hat, spilling his papers over the ground. Then the delighted children who had waited breathlessly in the bushes would rush out laughing and shouting to climb all over him. Abe, as pleased as the youngsters at the success of their harmless joke, always enjoyed such affectionate tomfoolery.

Lincoln made his living practicing law. But his passionate avocation was politics. After four terms in the state legislature, he felt that he was entitled to nomination by his fellow Whigs to a term in Congress. Denied this honor twice, he made an arrangement with the other district leaders of his party to be allowed his chance in 1846. In that year he was nominated by the Whigs, won neatly over his Democratic opponent, and, without feeling quite the joy he had anticipated in his victory, prepared to take his seat in the House of Representatives in December 1847.

The new and lone Whig congressman from Illinois and his rather pretty, somewhat plump, and frequently difficult wife made their long trip to Washington by steamboat and rail. The nation's capital in those days was a rambling town of some forty thousand people—thirty thousand white and ten thousand black residents. Of the latter, about one fifth were slaves. In fact the city supported the biggest slave market in the nation, actually within full view of the Capitol building itself.

In 1847 the seat of government had a temporary wooden dome and had not yet acquired its two present wings. On the White House lawn a marine band offered concerts for the populace on Wednesday and Sunday afternoons. But between the Executive Mansion and the river lay steaming malarial marshes. Pennsylvania Avenue was paved with large, uneven cobblestones over which the carriages of the wealthy bumped and rattled. Otherwise the streets were as unpaved as those of Springfield and as deep in mud or dust, depending on the weather. Here too were the familiar pigs, ducks, and geese feeding on the piles of garbage in the alleys. Mansions and shacks stood side by side in unzoned confusion.

If Lincoln felt little joy in winning the election, Mary was the one who was bitterly disappointed with the city of Washington. Despite her Kentucky heritage as a Todd, she had little social standing in the capital. The invitations she had expected were few and far between. The Lincolns took rooms at a boardinghouse which then occupied part of the area where the Library of Congress now stands. Abe almost immediately became a warm favorite of his messmates and bowling companions at the boardinghouse. They enjoyed his stories and his genial manner. Mary kept to her room except at mealtimes and made few friends. After some three months of this unpleasant life, she returned to her girlhood home in Kentucky to wait out her husband's first session in office.

It is this separation that gives us almost the only written evidence furnished by Abraham and Mary proving their love for each other. Four of Lincoln's letters and one of Mary's are preserved to show that, despite their frequent disagreements, they were fully capable of feeling lonesome for each other, and furthermore that they always shared an affectionate concern for the children.

What Lincoln wrote to his wife could hardly be called passionate love letters, but he did admit that he hated "to stay in this old room by myself." He had tried to find plaid stockings to fit "Eddy's dear little feet." He wanted Mary to enjoy herself "in every possible way." And he hoped his wife was "free from head-ache." He was afraid that Mary would be getting "so well, and fat, and young, as to be wanting to marry again." And he asked her to get weighed and tell him how much she weighed. Speaking of their sons, he said, "Don't let the blessed fellows forget father." And he signed himself "Most affectionately." If not lyrically romantic, such an epistle was at least a normally tender, domestic message from a husband to his wife.

When Lincoln took his seat as a freshman congressman far back in the House for the first session of the Thirtieth Congress, he was one of the least-known members of that legislative body. Within the chamber sat several men who had made history or were about to do so.

Most notable of all was the former president of

the United States, John Quincy Adams, a fellow Whig, eighty years old, shrewd, devoted to his country, and far more openly critical of slavery than Lincoln. By turning his head one way or another Abe could see Alexander H. Stephens of Georgia, who would one day be vice president of the Confederacy, and Andrew Johnson of Tennessee, later to be vice president of the United States under Lincoln. David Wilmot of Pennsylvania, one of the authors of the antislavery Wilmot Proviso, was perhaps the most controversial congressman on the floor. Not one of these men could have believed that by far the greatest among them was the gawky and green congressman from Illinois who never quite knew what to do with his big hands and feet.

There were many issues over which the Thirtieth Congress wrangled, but the most vexing were the Mexican War and the growing sectional dispute over slavery. Sometimes the two issues intertwined.

The war with Mexico was virtually over when Lincoln took his seat in 1847. But despite the victories the United States had enjoyed, a certain war weariness remained. Furthermore, President James K. Polk was a Democrat. This made him automatically unpopular with the Whigs.

Lincoln was busy on at least two important committees during his single term in Congress. But the only notice he was to receive, even in Illinois newspapers, concerned his sponsorship of the "spot resolutions" seeking to force President Polk to admit that the "spot" on which the first blood of the war was spilled was actually Mexican soil—thus branding Americans as the aggressors in an unrighteous conflict. Historians are still debating this very question. But it should be pointed out in passing that neither Lincoln nor the *Sangamo Journal* showed any desire to accept Mexican arrogance when the war began. And while Lincoln honestly hated war at all times during his life, his maneuver in this case also aided the strategy of the Whig party, which desired to make President Polk and the Democrats so unpopular that a Whig president could be elected in the next presidential election.

The more immediate effect of the "spot resolutions" was to make Abraham Lincoln one of the most unpopular men in Congress, even in his own state and congressional district. Many of Abe's friends and neighbors had been killed or wounded in the war. Billy Herndon pleaded with his partner in every letter to tone down his attacks. But Lincoln persisted in his antiwar, anti-Polk, anti-Democratic propaganda.

Once again, however, he did not devote himself solely to "practical politics." A bill that he drafted, seeking gradually to free the slaves of the District of Columbia, gave early national evidence of his desire to lessen this evil through conservative, nonviolent means. Nothing came of his effort.

After attending the second session, Lincoln returned to Springfield once again. Reestablished with Mary and the boys in their modest home, he hoped for some substantial appointive public office. But when he was offered the not very flattering post as Secretary of Oregon Territory, Mary, who had no desire to live in the far western wilderness, helped him make his decision against accepting it. Lincoln now felt he had destroyed forever his chance for a political career.

He returned rather sadly to his legal practice to spend several thoughtful, mellowing years. The Circuit Court of the Eighth Judicial District, which spread over nearly twelve thousand square miles of Illinois prairie land, furnished Lincoln a roving living that took him from one county seat to another, keeping him from home for weeks and even months at a time. Through driving blizzards, torrential rains, or clear and frosty weather, he rode the circuit.

Sometimes he straddled a plodding horse. Often he jogged along in a creaking buggy, his shawl drawn around his slightly stooping shoulders, a book forever in his hand. In the 1850s he sometimes traveled by rail. He mastered during these years most of the first six books of Euclid, believing rightly that geometry aids in the discipline of any mind. He read and memorized poetry.

At the various towns and villages where court was held, he met with the judge and other attorneys to spin yarns, argue politics, and joke through half the night. Lincoln was usually the life of the party, rousing from his melancholy to tell salty stories, droll anecdotes, and racy reminiscences. In court he could reduce his cases to the simplest and most convincing logic. And he won more legal battles than he lost. Nevertheless, for three continuous months he was beaten on virtually every occasion.

Lincoln had not yet reached the financial peak of his legal career, which was to come several years later when he collected his largest fee, a well-earned five thousand dollars from the Illinois Central Railroad. But perhaps it gave him more satisfaction to represent without fee a widow cheated out of half her government pension by an unscrupulous agent.

A later case for which he refused to accept a penny was his famous defense of Duff Armstrong, charged with murder. Young Armstrong was the son of Jack and Hannah Armstrong, Lincoln's friends from New Salem days. Witnesses swore that they had seen Duff in bright moonlight hit

James Metzker with a "slung shot." The principal witness so to swear was a house painter named Allen.

Lincoln was more than a "pretty good lawyer" on such occasions. He was brilliant.

Having listened to what he believed was perjury, Lincoln turned to the jury and said in effect, "Now I will show you that this man Allen's testimony is a pack of lies; that he never saw Armstrong strike Metzker with a slung shot; that he did not witness this fight by the light of the full moon, for the moon was not in the heavens that night."

Producing an almanac, Lincoln proved his point to the complete satisfaction of all concerned. The moon was not bright during the hour of that brawl, so Allen could not have seen what he said he had seen by "bright moonlight."

In his summation to the jury Lincoln carefully reviewed all the evidence of his client's innocence, ending on a note that could not help moving all who were present:

"Gentlemen, I appear here without any reward

for the benefit of that lady sitting there"—Lincoln indicated the weeping Hannah Armstrong, mother of Duff—"who washed my dirty shirts when I had no money to pay her." He told then of his young manhood in New Salem, and how the father and mother of Duff Armstrong had always furnished unstinted hospitality to a penniless young man who sometimes needed food and shelter. He believed that no son of such kind people could commit a murder.

Hannah Armstrong like Lincoln himself was overcome with emotion. The jury's decision to acquit the defendant confirmed Lincoln's strong conviction that Duff was innocent. When the "not guilty" verdict was returned, Lincoln said, "I pray to God that this lesson may prove in the end a good lesson to him and to all."

But the "Almanac Murder" was still some years in the future as Lincoln rode the circuit in the early 1850s through frost and fog, rain and sun.

Deep-eyed and thoughtful, ill-dressed, his high-water pantaloons seldom meeting his boots, a ridiculous sight in his short, yellow-flannel nightgown at the inns and taverns where he slept, Lincoln was studying, thinking, brooding, ripening toward the unforgettable statesman and humanitarian he was so soon to become.

11

A House Divided

I was losing interest in politics, when the repeal of the Missouri Compromise aroused me again.

A. LINCOLN

For more than forty years preceding the Civil War, sectional antagonism smoldered between the slave-holding southern states and the northern states, where slavery was forbidden. In 1820, when there were only twenty-two states in the Union—eleven slave and eleven free—a compromise was made to retain this balance. Maine was allowed to come into the Union as a free state. Missouri was brought in as a slave state.

However, one of the most important provisions

of this famous "Missouri Compromise" was the "sacred pledge" that within that part of the Louisiana Purchase not yet admitted to statehood and also lying north of the line 36° 30′, slavery was to be forever excluded.

In January 1854, Lincoln's old nemesis Senator Stephen A. Douglas introduced a bill in the Senate that rocked the entire nation and sharply increased the ill feeling between the North and the South. This bill, the Kansas–Nebraska Act, would repeal the Missouri Compromise and raise again the whole bitter question as to what limits (if any) were to be placed on the further extension of slavery.

The Douglas proposal, which was finally accepted by both houses of Congress after months of angry debate, allowed the citizens of the Territory of Kansas and the Territory of Nebraska (both north of the agreed line) to determine for themselves whether they wished to be admitted as free states or slave. Men like Lincoln, who feared the further spread of slavery, felt that the new act violated the "sacred pledge" that this area would be forever free.

Kansas almost immediately became the scene of violent clashes between proslavery and antislavery pioneers. They rushed into the territory on horseback and in covered wagons, armed with rifles and Bowie knives, each group wishing to dominate any election in which slavery sentiment might be tested.

But even before the looting, shooting, and burning began in "Bleeding Kansas," the war of words concerning the new act spread over the entire nation. Lincoln could not watch this struggle on an issue so vitally important without adding his own voice and logic to the debate. He saw his old, conciliatory Whig party split and destroyed by the clash. He watched a new and vigorous party made up of men who called themselves "Republicans" gain converts every day by its outspoken resistance to the further spread of slavery.

And although Lincoln was slow to join these "radical" Republicans, he was less slow to attack the Kansas–Nebraska Act.

Lincoln ran for the United States Senate and was defeated by the vote of the Illinois legislature on February 8, 1855. (In those days, United States senators were elected by their state legislatures.)

By the following year, Lincoln realized that he must cast his lot with the Republicans if he wished to be effective in fighting the growing evil. By May 29, 1856, there was no longer any doubt where Lincoln stood on the great issue then racking the nation. On that date in Bloomington, at the official birth of the Republican Party of Illinois, he made a speech so overwhelming in its effect that he virtually hypnotized his audience. Even the newspaper reporters were so spellbound that they forgot to take notes. His powerful address thus became the famous and tantalizing "Lost Speech."

Billy Herndon, who sat entranced, later wrote: "I have heard or read all of Mr. Lincoln's great speeches, and I give it as my opinion that the Bloomington speech was the grand effort of this life. Heretofore he had simply argued the slavery question on grounds of policy—the statesman's grounds—never reaching the question of . . . the eternal right. Now he was newly baptized and freshly born; he had the fervor of a new convert; the smothered flame broke out; enthusiasm unusual to him blazed up; his eyes were aglow with an inspiration."

Herndon, who in those days always took notes on Lincoln's speeches, soon tossed aside his pen and paper and "lived only in the inspiration of the hour." He, like the others about him, was mesmerized by the fire, energy, and force of Lincoln's great address. He found these winged words filled with tough truths, however, "hard, heavy, knotty, gnarly backed with wrath." Abraham Lincoln was taking a wrestler's grip on the enemy. As Herndon put it, "If Mr. Lincoln was six feet four inches high usually, at Bloomington that day he was seven feet, and inspired at that."

Although no authenticated version of the speech survives, news of its effect on that assemblage of Illinois Republicans must have spread eastward rapidly. At the Republican National Convention in Philadelphia three weeks later, where delegates were gathered to choose their first presidential slate, Lincoln was given 110 votes for the vice presidential nomination. Thus he had an outside chance of becoming the running mate of the presidential nominee, John C. Frémont. Later voting eliminated Lincoln and gave vice presidential honors to William L. Dayton of New Jersey.

When Lincoln was told of the 110 votes, he said in wry amazement: "I reckon that ain't me; there's another great man in Massachusetts named Lincoln, and I reckon it's him."

It was fortunate that Lincoln was not the vice presidential nominee on that first rather weak Republican ticket. It is even more fortunate, in the light of later history, that Frémont was beaten by the weak-willed Democratic candidate, James Buchanan. The South was already threatening secession in the event that Frémont reached the White House. This might well have proved fatal to the nation. For in 1856 the North was not sufficiently united to have successfully resisted such a secession.

Only two days after Buchanan was inaugurated to the presidency, the United States Supreme Court, under Chief Justice Roger B. Taney of Maryland, handed down the Dred Scott decision, ruling that a black man "is so far inferior to a white man" that he could not be considered a citizen in a court of law. This further inflamed antislavery elements in the North as the cold war between the two sections became increasingly warm.

Lincoln's race for the Senate in 1858 was a far more serious effort than he had made four years previously. Senator Douglas, now approaching the end of his second term, was to be his opponent. The fact that Lincoln was facing such a famous and powerful adversary made this a major battle.

In accepting his nomination before the Republican State Convention in Springfield on June 16, 1858, Lincoln made a speech for which he hoped he might be remembered if all else were erased from his record. It was the "House Divided" speech, so utterly frank and fearless that his friends, except Herndon, pleaded with him not to give it. Herndon, however, said prophetically: "Lincoln, deliver that speech as read and it will make you president!"

Here are the warning words from that address, which still ring like a solemn bell:

" 'A house divided against itself cannot stand.' I believe this government cannot endure, permanently half *slave* and half *free*. I do not expect the Union to be *dissolved*—I do not expect the house to *fall*—but I *do* expect it will cease to be divided."

Those words, which gave courage to many in the North, stirred deep anger in the South. They were soon being twisted by Stephen A. Douglas in an effort to prove that Lincoln desired to foment a civil war. Douglas, that wily master of political controversy, asked for nothing more damaging than Lincoln's own declaration on this delicate issue. And Douglas knew that he would need all such ammunition if he were to defeat his tall and rangy opponent. He did not underrate his adversary. When Douglas first heard of Lincoln's nomination for the Senate, he said that of all the Whigs about Springfield, "Abe Lincoln is the ablest and the most honest."

The return of Douglas to Illinois to stump the state for his reelection was something of a triumphal tour. The wealthy, influential, and cocky "Little Giant" customarily traveled from town to town in a private railroad car with his beautiful and socially accomplished second wife, Adele

Cutts Douglas, whose smart wardrobe was the talk of the nation's capital (not to mention rural Illinois). One of the cars of the train was a flatcar on which was mounted a gleaming brass cannon attended by men in uniform. This cannon was fired as the train pulled into any town to announce to the citizens that the great Stephen A. Douglas was arriving to make an address. Often riding in one of the dingy passenger cars behind the same engine was the tall, rather disheveled Abe Lincoln, who had neither the money nor the desire to rival the conspicuous display of his opponent. Each candidate had certain advantages in his particular brand of appeal. But as Lincoln is said to have remarked: "You can fool all the people some of the time, and some of the people all the time, but you cannot fool all the people all the time."

At first Lincoln merely followed the senator from one town to another, speaking in rebuttal when called on by the audience or addressing independently staged assemblies. Then it occurred to him that it would be more effective and convenient if they shared the same platform. Lincoln challenged Douglas to a series of debates, and Douglas, who had little to gain and much to lose by such an arrangement, nevertheless accepted the challenge.

This is how it happened that seven Illinois towns—Ottawa, Freeport, Jonesboro, Charleston, Galesburg, Quincy, and Alton—were honored by Lincoln and Douglas as the scenes of their "great debates," so influential in the shaping of American history.

The crowds came by boat, oxcart, horse and buggy, special excursion trains, and afoot. They saw torchlight processions, uniformed brass bands, and floats blooming with pretty girls. They gazed at the flags, bunting, and slogans, ate and drank the refreshments. They stood in the hot sun at Ottawa, in the drizzling rain at Freeport, and in chilly gales at Galesburg. Entranced, spellbound, entertained, annoyed, or delighted, they cheered, laughed, listened, and cheered again. Not even P. T. Barnum could have provided them with a better show.

Douglas was dapper, usually wearing a blue or

white coat, frilled shirt, low-cut waistcoat, well-tailored trousers, and polished boots. He was an aggressive, assured, and eloquent debater, sly as a fox, slippery as an eel. Lincoln, towering a full twelve inches above this mighty midget, wore his rusty black coat with sleeves too short to reach his wrists, a shirt that always seemed rumpled, and a tie that was always awry. He usually carried an old gray shawl and a bulging umbrella. But when either of these men began to speak, the thousands swarming around the platform soon forgot their physical appearance, forgot the broiling heat or the bitter chill, as two of the greatest debaters of their era brought the full power of their lucid minds to bear upon their subject.

If Douglas was a fox, Lincoln was a foxhound. At Freeport, Abe asked a skillfully devised question: How can the people of a territory legally "exclude slavery from its limits prior to the formation of a state constitution?" Lincoln knew the answer that Douglas would give. And he rightly assumed that this would eventually destroy the senator's presidential aspirations, whether or not it spelled the senator's downfall in the current campaign.

Said Douglas, almost glibly, any territory that wished to eliminate slavery could do so by passing laws "unfriendly" to that institution. A roar of delight swept through the audience—but this appeal to the sentiments of many Northern voters infuriated most Southern Democrats. Douglas's famous response, which became known as the Freeport Doctrine, cost him about one third of his political backing and eventually split the Democratic party, making the Republican presidential victory of 1860 almost inevitable.

At each of the seven gatherings, newspaper reporters took down "full phonographic verbatim reports" in shorthand. Therefore, not only the eager crowds at each debate, but readers all over the United States were able to follow every word of the controversy. Almost overnight Abraham Lincoln became famous and a power to be reckoned with in national politics.

But after those exhausting hours on the platform, when Lincoln was able to take off his tie and his shoes in his hotel room, a different mood came over him as he sat alone with his thoughts. The humorist David R. Locke, better known by his pen name Petroleum V. Nasby, talked to Lincoln as he relaxed one evening at Quincy. Said Locke, "I never saw a more thoughtful face. I never saw a more dignified face. I never saw so sad a face."

Lincoln told Locke that he hoped to carry the state on the popular vote, but that—as in 1855—he did not expect to defeat Douglas in the state legislature. He explained to Locke that through a political maneuver known as gerrymandering, many election districts had been cleverly mapped to give unfair advantage to his opponents, the Democrats.

Once again Lincoln proved prophetic. When that rainy election day of November 2, 1858, rolled around, Lincoln's supporters received 125,275 popular votes while Douglas's allies received 121,090. But when the legislature met to choose a senator, fifty-four assemblymen voted for Douglas and only forty-six for Lincoln.

When asked how he felt about his defeat, Lincoln told the story of a barefooted boy who stubbed his toe. "It hurt too bad to laugh, and he was too big to cry."

In spite of this new misfortune, Lincoln remained a figure of interest to citizens throughout the country. During the next year and a half he labored to repair his legal business, which he had sadly neglected during most of the year of 1858. He still made speeches, but not always political ones. Despite the fact that he began to be mentioned for the presidency, he was reluctant even to dream of such high office. To one newspaper editor who was prepared to back him vigorously, Lincoln replied, "I must, in candor, say I do not think myself fit for the presidency."

But during the early autumn of 1859 his views were slowly changing on this subject. In a letter written to Lyman Trumbull on April 29, 1860, Lincoln said of the proffered political plum, "The taste *is* in my mouth a little." However, he asked Trumbull to let no other eye see the letter.

This change of heart and hope was doubtless partly due to the excellent reception of Lincoln's important speech at Cooper Union in New York City and the wild applause that greeted him during his unscheduled tour through New England. It is also evident that Lincoln was carefully analyzing the possibilities of the other chief contenders for the Republican presidential nomination and was finding certain important weaknesses in the chances of each. William H. Seward of New York, Salmon P. Chase of Ohio, Simon Cameron of Pennsylvania, and two prominent jurists—John McLean, a United States Supreme Court justice from Ohio, and Edward Bates of Missouri—were all possible choices. But each of these men, including William H. Seward, who was by far the favorite, either lacked support in certain key regions of the North or had alienated possible voters by statements too radical or forthright to live down.

Lincoln's moderate position on slavery had a wider popular appeal. Despite unfounded charges by Douglas and others, Lincoln had no desire to dismember the Union over the slavery issue. And he definitely was *not* an Abolitionist. His shrewd mind must have grasped the fact that his chances would be good at the Republican National Convention. Certainly there could be no doubt that he was the "favorite son" of his own state. This had

135

been proved dramatically at the Illinois Republican Convention in Decatur, where every vote had gone to Lincoln. The high moment of that gathering came when John Hanks and a friend had marched in carrying two rails supposedly split by Abe when he had first come to Macon County thirty years previous. The delegates went mad with joy. Abe the "Rail Splitter" would be a likely vote getter throughout the North and West.

When the Republicans came pouring into Chicago for their national convention on May 16, 1860, excitement mounted. Some delegates, such as Seward's, brought with them huge bands in bright uniforms. The "Wide Awakes," whose candidate was Abe Lincoln, gathered from everywhere to march up and down Michigan Avenue, making almost as much noise as Seward's band. They wore capes and caps fashioned from oilcloth, which shimmered in the sun during the day and gleamed in the light of the kerosene torches that they carried at night.

But while the singing, band playing, and cheering echoed along the Chicago lakefront, serious scheming was afoot in the smoke-filled hotel rooms. Managers for all the major candidates were pulling every conceivable trick from their political bags to gain victory by fair means or foul. Among the most astute were Thurlow Weed, political boss of New York, fighting for Seward, and Simon Cameron, the political boss of Pennsylvania, fighting for himself.

Lincoln chose to stay in Springfield. But his managers, headed by huge and jovial Judge David Davis, who had ridden the circuit with Lincoln, were just as busy and just as conniving as any of their opponents.

Lincoln sent a message to his managers: "Make no contracts that will bind me."

"Honest Abe," waiting patiently in Springfield, perhaps did not realize what his devoted friends were enduring in his behalf. Contracts definitely *were* made, including such important promises as cabinet posts in the new administration. But good *did* come of this political maneuvering. American citizens were spared the irreparable loss they would have suffered had Lincoln been defeated. The finest possible leader was being chosen for one of the most dangerous and exacting terms of office ever held by an American president.

The interest of all delegates now centered on the Wigwam, a huge, flimsily built wooden building erected for the express purpose of housing the convention. Tightly crammed, this firetrap rocked and roared with the usual fantastic hullabaloo that is typical of political conventions. Nominating speeches in those days were mercifully brief. In a very short time the delegates were voting.

The first ballot gave Seward 173½ votes, Lincoln 102, Cameron 50½, Chase 49, Bates 48. There were also 42 votes scattered among other contenders.

"Call the roll! Call the roll!" roared the convention.

The second ballot gave Lincoln 181, but Seward still led him by three and one-half votes.

"Call the roll! Call the roll!" screamed the delegates.

Only 233 votes were needed to clinch the nomination. On the third roll call, Lincoln's tally climbed until it reached 231½, only one and one-half votes from victory.

Up jumped an Ohio delegate. He was recognized by the chair.

"I rise (eh), Mr. Chairman (eh), to announce the change of four votes of Ohio from Mr. Chase to Mr. Lincoln."

Now pandemonium really broke loose as the delegates cheered, roared, whistled, and tossed hats and bunting into the air. A signal was given to a man waiting on the roof, who pulled the lanyard on the victory cannon.

At the office of the *Illinois State Journal* in Springfield, Lincoln and some of his friends were waiting with what patience they could muster. Suddenly the telegram arrived: "We did it. Glory to God."

As his loyal neighbors danced, cheered, sang, pumped his hand, and patted one another on the back, Lincoln said quietly, "Well, gentlemen, there is a little short woman at our house who is probably more interested in this dispatch than I am; and if you will excuse me, I will take it up and let her see it."

It is never possible to predict the outcome of an election with one hundred percent assurance. But with the Democratic Party split wide open (thanks partly to Lincoln's crafty maneuver at Freeport), the Republican chances looked excellent. Stephen A. Douglas was the nominee of the Northern Democrats. John C. Breckinridge was the choice of the Southern Democrats. No one seemed particularly worried about John Bell, backed by a party that called itself the Constitutional Union.

When that historic election day dawned on November 6, 1860, amid the threats of secession in the South, the citizens streamed into the polling places, tense with excitement and well aware that more than an election was in the wind.

Lincoln won, not by a majority, it is true, but by a healthy plurality. The final tally showed 1,866,452 for Lincoln; 1,376,957 for Douglas; 849,781 for Breckinridge; and 588,879 for Bell. Thus Lincoln was the final winner in his long debate with Douglas.

Humble Abe Lincoln born in a log cabin had proved once again that America actually *is* the land of opportunity. Ahead of him lay such responsibilities as few have ever carried upon their shoulders. Lincoln would grow in mind and heart and soul to be worthy of that great load. Ahead of him lay the glory and the tragedy of being the leader of his people in a heartbreaking civil war. He was the new president of the United States of America. And now there was no doubt that Mary Lincoln would have her wish. She would be mistress of the White House—the first lady of the land.

12

With Malice Toward None

I bid you an affectionate farewell.

A. LINCOLN

He had roped the trunks and boxes himself and had addressed them to "A. Lincoln, The White House, Washington, D.C." The Springfield residence was rented; a new home had been found for the dog. The horse and cow had been sold. He had paid a last visit to his beloved stepmother, Sarah Bush Lincoln. And he had told Billy Herndon to let their shingle hang undisturbed. There would be no change in the firm of Lincoln and Herndon. "If I live I'm coming back some time, and then we'll go right on practicing law as if nothing had ever happened."

Those were the homely details of departure. But in the rare moments he had to himself, Lincoln realized that his country was trembling on the brink of civil war—often as he might deny that terrifying fact. The president-elect was prayerfully determined to prevent the horror of such mass bloodshed if, by any honorable means, it could be avoided.

A cold rain was falling on that dismal morning of February 11, 1861, when Lincoln and his party made their way to the little brick railroad station of the Great Western, where a small engine attached to a baggage car, smoking car, and one passenger coach made up the Presidential Special.

Standing on the rear platform, Lincoln peered out over the sea of umbrellas and the upturned faces.

"My friends," he said quietly, "no one not in my situation can appreciate my feeling of sadness at this parting. To this place, and the kindness of these people, I owe every thing. Here I have lived a quarter of a century, and have passed from a young to an old man. Here my children have been born, and one is buried. I now leave, not knowing when, or whether ever, I may return, with a task before me greater than that which rested upon Washington. Without the assistance of that Divine Being, Who ever attended him, I cannot succeed. With that assistance I cannot fail. Trusting in Him, Who can go with me, and remain with you and be every where for good, let us confidently hope that all will yet be well. To His care commending you, as I hope in your prayers you will commend me, I bid you an affectionate farewell."

The whistle of the little engine wailed, the bell clanged, and the train disappeared slowly into the mist, headed toward the distant capital of a troubled nation.

Although Lincoln was known for his kindliness and his hatred of cruelty, injustice, and war, nevertheless war soon became inevitable. After the Confederate guns fired on Fort Sumter on April 12, 1861, the rival armies of the North and South began to gather under their generals for the tragic and bloody four-year struggle.

The volunteers of these two armies differed little in idealism and courage; average weight and height; color of hair, skin, eyes; love of family and country. They left behind them weeping mothers and proud fathers, women with whom they were in love. With an ardor that might better have been spent on binding North and South together, these bearded young men and beardless striplings threw themselves at each other with fratricidal fury. At times they even cheered the bravery of those who came on against them.

The great guns roared, spewing grapeshot, ball, and shrapnel into the advancing tides of Blue and Gray. From behind stone walls and earthworks came the rattle of the musketry. Men charged with fixed bayonets, fell groaning, died or were carried to the rear. The endless war rolled on.

The congressmen and their ladies came out to see the First Battle of Bull Run as though it were a picnic. But when the southern General Jackson stood like a "Stonewall," and when the Union advance became first a retreat and then a rout, these gentlemen and their ladies fought frantically to drive their smart rigs through the wild mob racing for Washington. The country was discovering that war is not a picnic.

By 1862 there were few illusions on either side. During the Peninsular Campaign, the fighting in the Shenandoah Valley, and at such bloody battles as Second Bull Run, Antietam, and Fredericksburg, the casualties were appalling.

By 1863 the tide began to turn against the Confederacy. Their slaves had been declared by Lincoln "thenceforward, and forever *FREE*." Vicksburg fell to Union troops after a period of siege. Despite heroic fighting, Lee's forces were turned back at Gettysburg.

Lincoln, who had tried McDowell, McClellan, Burnside, Hooker, and Meade, finally found his general in Ulysses S. Grant. During 1864 this cigar-smoking, whisky-drinking master of merciless assault fought ferocious engagements in the wilderness, at Spotsylvania Courthouse, Cold Harbor, and around Richmond and Petersburg before starting his long siege of the Confederate capital. Meanwhile Sherman was cutting a fiery swath through Georgia to the sea.

Above the thunder of guns, a wise and tender voice was often heard. It was the voice of Abraham Lincoln, trying even during the fury of battle to lessen the hatred.

The great voice said:

"In *giving* freedom to the *slave,* we *assure* freedom to the *free.*"

Again it said:

"Four score and seven years ago our fathers brought forth on this continent, a new nation, conceived in Liberty, and dedicated to the proposition that all men are created equal. Now we are engaged in a great civil war, testing whether that nation, or any nation so conceived and so dedicated, can long endure."

And finally, only a little more than a month before that voice was to be silenced forever, came words more majestic than any that were ever uttered by the head of a government during a time of desperate conflict:

"With malice toward none; with charity for all; with firmness in the right, as God gives us to see the right, let us strive on to finish the work we are in; to bind up the nation's wounds; to care for him who shall have borne the battle, and for his widow, and his orphan—to do all which may achieve and cherish a just, and a lasting peace, among ourselves, and with all nations."

As Lincoln proclaimed this doctrine of charity in his Second Inaugural Address on that day of wind and rain, March 4, 1865, the sun broke through the clouds and shone directly on him. To some in the audience, this seemed a sign and a portent. They felt that through the clouds of war the sun of hope was shining upon a broken and struggling nation.

When at last the gallant Robert E. Lee and his weary troops—lacking food, medical supplies, and ammunition—were forced to surrender to Ulysses S. Grant at Appomattox Court House on April 9, 1865, the Union had been saved, but at what a terrible cost! In the North, a great quavering sigh of relief and joy swept across farms, villages, and cities. Even in the South, despite all the bitterness of defeat, there was now a certain release from pain. The war was over.

But almost before President Lincoln could grasp the blessed fact that the guns were no longer firing, he was cut down by an assassin's bullet at Ford's Theater in Washington while he sat in his box with his wife watching a play called *Our American Cousin.* The bullet, fired from an eight-ounce brass derringer held in the hand of the crazed actor John Wilkes Booth, ended the life of the frontier boy who had risen from poverty and ignorance and illiteracy to become one of the greatest, the most profound, and the most merciful leaders the world has ever known. Had Lincoln lived, he might have saved his country from much of the bitterness that marked the years of Reconstruction to follow. For it is certain that he would have repudiated vengeance on the defeated South. He wished only to "bind up the nation's wounds." His loss was the loss of every citizen North and South of whatever creed or color. In his death they were deprived of a great healer and mediator who had "malice toward none; with charity for all."

As Lincoln had said when leaving Springfield, he did not know "when, or whether ever," he might return. But now in a train draped with mourning, through cities, towns, and villages where weeping thousands stood through the April days and nights to pay their last tribute, Abe Lincoln of Illinois was returning to his home, there to sleep peacefully until Judgment Day.

And every April, when the lilacs bloom, he will be remembered.